Jimmie Durham, Europe, and the Art of Relations

This book investigates Jimmie Durham's community-building process of making and display in four of his projects in Europe: *Something … Perhaps a Fugue or an Elegy* (2005); two Neapolitan nativities (2016 and ongoing); *The Middle Earth* (with Maria Thereza Alves, 2018); and *God's Poems, God's Children* (2017).

Andrea Feeser explores these artworks in the context of ideas about connection set forth by writers Ann Lauterbach, Franz Rosenzweig, Pamela Sue Anderson, Vinciane Despret, and Hirokazu Miyazaki, among others. Feeser argues that the materials in Durham's artworks; the method of their construction; how Durham writes about his pieces; how they exist with respect to one another; and how they address viewers demonstrate that we can create alongside others a world that embraces and sustains what has been diminished.

The book will be of interest to scholars working in contemporary art, animal studies, new materialism research, and eco-criticism.

Andrea Feeser is Professor of Modern and Contemporary Art History, Theory, and Criticism at Clemson University.

Routledge Focus on Art History and Visual Studies

Jimmie Durham, Europe, and the Art of Relations

Andrea Feeser

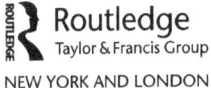

Routledge
Taylor & Francis Group

NEW YORK AND LONDON

First published 2021
by Routledge
52 Vanderbilt Avenue, New York, NY 10017

and by Routledge
2 Park Square, Milton Park, Abingdon, Oxon, OX14 4RN

Routledge is an imprint of the Taylor & Francis Group, an informa business

© 2021 Taylor & Francis

Library of Congress Cataloging-in-Publication Data
Names: Feeser, Andrea, author.
Title: Jimmie Durham, Europe, and the art of relations / Andrea Feeser.
Description: New York: Routledge, 2021. | Includes bibliographical references and index.
Identifiers: LCCN 2020025254 (print) | LCCN 2020025255 (ebook) | ISBN 9780367404550 (hardback) | ISBN 9780429356230 (ebook)
Subjects: LCSH: Durham, Jimmie—Criticism and interpretation.
Classification: LCC N6537.D875 F44 2021 (print) | LCC N6537.D875 (ebook) | DDC 709.2—dc23
LC record available at https://lccn.loc.gov/2020025254
LC ebook record available at https://lccn.loc.gov/2020025255

ISBN: 978-0-367-40455-0 (hbk)
ISBN: 978-0-367-54881-0 (pbk)
ISBN: 978-0-429-35623-0 (ebk)

Typeset in Times New Roman
by codeMantra

In honor of dafalcon

Contents

Figures

Preface – On Relations

Writers seek the right words in the right combinations to express, move, convey, persuade, and/or motivate, and artists do something similar with their materials in compositions. For both creators, this entails striking some sort of balance or productive tension among different elements that are tangible, intangible, factual, subjective, conclusive, and inconclusive. For writers, and most artists, it also means finding words for that which exceeds them. If these efforts generate interest, discussion and debate ensue. People who take up art evaluate it in terms of how they understand its aesthetic and ethos, and what these qualities in tandem accomplish; this involves the circumstances and experiences that have shaped their thinking and tenets, both of which are deeply intertwined. I see this as the art of relations, the heart and mind of creation and reception, a dynamic through which people tussle with making and meaning and form communities of shared understanding and conviction. Affective, cognitive, and political, I think the art of relations is dialogic and agonistic, a subconscious or conscious politics with varying stakes and consequences for people who believe that art impacts them and others for whom they care.

In *Jimmie Durham, Europe, and the Art of Relations*, I address dimensions of these configurations in some of Durham's recent art and writing in Europe. Durham's work asks viewers and readers to think with him in specific circumstances about what they and others value and devalue, and what this suggests. I find this important because I believe that self-reflective knowledge about significance grounds informed, careful, and open exchanges with others that are receptive to critique and transformation, and which may guide positive action. I greatly value the work of exploring in situated conditions other ways of knowing and being that sharpen intellect and ethics. I believe that this creates opportunities for people to welcome difference and engage justice within communities they occupy. My students, most of whom are artists, live the conviction that art is not for its own sake alone. It is a sort of philosophy. Philosophy is sometimes described as a method for living a good life. In the abstract, this can mean anything. In particular instances of art, like those I discuss in this book, I believe that it is an opportunity to think with others about what might and can be right in the arenas that affect us and that we affect.

Notes on Language

When referencing artists and scholars, I identify them with respect to their practices, and to their identities and/or citizenship if they do so. When writing of Native peoples and their projects, I use terminology recommended by Robert Warrior, Hall Distinguished Professor of American Literature and Culture at the University of Kansas and a member/citizen of the Osage Nation.

First, I employ "the names that specific tribal groups have for themselves ... or at least the names by which they have come to be known since the European colonization of the Americas," and then American Indian as a noun with Indian and Native as adjectives.*

When I use the terms Europe, European, Euro-American, and Eurocentric, I include Britain and British inheritances as and from Western Europe, the part of the Eurasian continent typically defined as Europe.

When I write "we" without qualifiers, I address you, a reader I think is someone involved with art and its circumstances in some way, and do so in the context of proposing a scenario within which I hope you see yourself.

---

* Warrior, Robert. 2014. "Indian." In *Keywords for American Cultural Studies*, 2nd ed., edited by Bruce Burgett and Glen Hendler. New York: New York University Press. https://keywords.nyupress.org/american-cultural-studies/essay/indian/.

Acknowledgments

I am grateful for research support from both Clemson University's Division of Research and College of Architecture, Arts and Humanities, and for writing support from the university's Art Department Chair Valerie Zimany, who gave me a fall 2019 course release. I thank Heike Munder, Director of the Migros Museum für Gegenwartskunst and Nathalie Ergino, Director of the Institut d'art Contemporain, Villeurbanne for including me in events surrounding the exhibitions *God's Children, God's Poems* and *The Middle Earth*; they enabled me to study artworks carefully and discuss with audiences their reactions to the works. I also thank José Kuri, kurimanzutto co-founder and Richard William Hill, Canada Research Chair in Indigenous Studies at Emily Carr University of Art + Design for sharing their insights into Durham's work with me. I greatly appreciate guidance I received from Clemson University's Rhondda Thomas, Calhoun Lemon Professor of Literature; Lee Morrisey, Founding Director of the Clemson Humanities Hub and Alumni Distinguished Professor of English; Walt Hunter, Associate Professor of World Literature; Matt Hooley, Assistant Professor and Environmental Humanities, Native American Studies, and US Colonialism scholar; and artist Lori Johnson, MFA student in Drawing. Artists Haley Floyd and Kevin Pohle provided me with thoughtful perspectives on and wonderful images of Durham's practice, and Durham's Studio Manager Kai-Morten Vollmer gave me excellent exposure to the workings of Durham's studios. Editor Isabella Vitti and Editorial Assistant Katie Armstrong of Routledge Press made work on my manuscript very gratifying, as did my anonymous readers. I thank *Religion and the Arts* for permitting me to use portions of an article I published with the journal.*

* Feeser, Andrea. 2019. "Neighbors and Faith in Community: Artist Jimmie Durham's Neapolitan *Presepi*." *Religion and the Arts* 23, no. 4: 516–36.

At home, my husband Tim Factor and son Noah Factor gave me warm support, as did from afar my parents Robert and Elaine Feeser and sister Hilarey Bhatt. My students, who are artists for whom I wrote this book, served as my inspiration, and my artist and scholar interlocutors in this text taught and continue to teach me many important lessons. Jimmie Durham and Maria Thereza Alves shared their great intellects and powerful art with me, as well as generous hospitality. My sincere thanks to all of you.

Introduction – Art Exists for Us Socially

Artist, poet, essayist, and activist Jimmie Durham's five-decade career investigates European and American worldviews and institutions in the contexts of politics and culture. Durham questions and undermines narratives and structures that uphold unjust Eurocentric ideas and practices. He does so by putting building blocks of communication such as physical materials, language, and bodily expression into surprising and often humorous relationships that subvert hierarchy, logic, and belief. Durham's work is not didactic: it does not produce stable meaning nor deliver an unequivocal message. Conscious that a will to do so would replace one ideological imperative with another, Durham courts confusion and welcomes interruption. His performances, writings, installations, and objects solicit attention through unobtrusive wit, invite investigation through surprising juxtaposition, encourage political analysis with critical content, and engage self-reflection with intellectual rigor.

In 2014, Durham published a short essay about his longstanding and ongoing art making with wood. As with the rest of his writing, in this piece, he carefully chose his words and their delivery. Durham's language in the essay is descriptive, concrete, chiefly realistic, and humorous when a bit fantastic. He first recounts a natural history of the earth, focusing on how trees around the world enrich other beings, and then sets forth a history of his involvement with different types of wood, emphasizing their communicative properties. Durham names what and whom he has worked alongside: specific woods, as well as people closely involved with their particular communities, whose feet he says rest "solidly on the ground." He views this state as "the only basis for intellectuality" and writes with admiration of an Italian artist-geologist who identified for Durham the stones they encountered on walks (2014).

Durham's essay appears in the Italian contemporary art publication *Mousse Magazine*, and it features photographs of several artworks with wood the artist produced, including those exhibited in 2012 at Naples' luxurious Palazzo Reale. Part of the show *Stone, Wood, and Friends*, the creations' elegant, raw materiality stands in stark contrast to the palace's dazzling, virtuoso construction and decoration. The building complex draws thousands of visitors keen to learn about Naples' royal past, and *Mousse Magazine* attracts hundreds of readers interested in cutting-edge art from around the globe. At each rarified site, palace and contemporary art magazine, Durham inserts straightforward yet idiosyncratic constructions of materials, physical in the first case and textual in the second. These sharp juxtapositions prod those of us who examine art and sites of visual culture to reflect on what we value, how we relate, where we place ourselves, and why we consider these phenomena the ways that we do. Do we prefer gnarled wood with bone displayed as sculpture to gold decor dispersed throughout palatial architecture? Are we comfortable with odd musings about wood published next to specialized art criticism? Do we fit comfortably or awkwardly in unusual and/or expected places for art? If we think about these and other things while reflecting on the artist's use of wood, it's because we answer "yes" to the question Durham poses as the title of his essay about it: "Is This Interesting?"

Interest is a basic condition necessary to engage others in many pursuits. Durham's question acknowledges this and therefore the possibility that what he thinks and produces as an artist and writer may have no purchase. This perspective rarely appears in art world discourse and practice: typically, it is a given that an artwork, exhibition, or essay merits time and energy. Questions certainly arise within and about art projects, but after significance is assumed or stated. Durham's question presumes nothing and is thus open: it solicits thinking but makes a place for refusal. In this short book about several recent art projects Durham produced in Europe, I attempt something similar. Like "Is This Interesting?" I recount, describe, marshal what may seem fantastic, opine, and acknowledge those who impact my work and why I value them. However, unlike Durham in "Is This Interesting?" who frames scenarios for critical thought, I do so *and* invest in persuasion. I believe that Durham's current art in Europe asks us to think about what is discarded and built up there to make and break communities in and of place, and to consider what this means more broadly. I argue that thinking about this deeply addresses what we value and our values, and asks us to assume responsibility for how and why we connect with those we do, wherever we are, toward the ends we seek. I want my readers to say "yes" to what I maintain. By contrast, Durham's work always troubles conviction and keeps the possibility of refusal at its core. Ironically, as I build a case for why Durham's recent art merits attention, it is his commitment to destabilizing pronouncements and making room for "no" that I argue matters a great deal.

This condition of Durham's practice begs the question – where does he stand? He says "at the center of the world" when talking about staffs he has created to mark it. This suggests conceit until we recognize that Durham does not produce these staffs at one site, nor does he wield them like a scepter. He makes them for places to which he has been invited, and at these locations, he stands alongside, not in front of, the people and other entities he encounters within their environments – *their* centers. Because Durham left the US, where he was born, challenges the authority of nation-states, and has traveled to and lived in places where he was asked to work, he describes himself as a "world citizen" who is stateless. Since he shows art in varied places, many of which are renowned art venues, this invokes the specter of the star artist who jets from one art fair, biennial, gallery, museum, and triennial to the next on the glamorous art world circuit. However, we would only see this single trajectory if we failed to look elsewhere: to less visible sites where Durham works like his Neapolitan neighborhood that I discuss in this book. Considering this place in relation to well-known art venues at which he exhibits, we can observe comparisons and contrasts Durham produces that undercut hierarchy, and notice the opportunity to reflect on where we see value, and how we might experience it. Moreover, what our decisions or equivocations about this suggest.

In the broadest sense, troubling categories and established systems of value has been and remains the work of those who want to change the realms they occupy. This is especially evident in the world of politics writ large, such as battles today that play out in and around climate change, but it is clear in the art world too, where iconoclasts defy conventions operating around their work. To an extent, constant innovation has itself become a convention in experimental art and other practices where new formations accrue value, especially when monetized. It is therefore possible to see Durham's challenges to rules and regulations as part of an art system that tames and institutionalizes the best efforts of many in the arts who propose new and supposedly improved ways of doing things. When art today is bought and sold often at great expense, and experienced as an elite pursuit by many who revel in or revile the specialized languages it requires, it certainly seems incapable of shifting paradigms in any pronounced manner. However, if we who take up art perceive it as Durham does, as a form of thought that does intellectual work, perhaps art is not only economic and cultural capital, but also critical ideas and propositions formed by means less concrete than typical modalities for thought such as rational oral and written communication. We often find it extremely hard to put an experience of art into words, including art produced by words, such as poetry. However, in trying to do this, we think, stretch our thinking, and may turn to others to test our thought, and extend it further. This is what I take Durham to mean when he says, "art exists for us socially" (2017, 11). In addition, this is a nexus where I maintain that something unconventional and perhaps better can happen if we find Durham's practice interesting, and do not say "no" by turning away from it. Few people in the art world have turned away from Durham's work, although in the early 1990s and recently, during his 2017–18 North American retrospective, some argued that one should. I think this argument contributes to the work of assessing value and values that Durham's art puts into play.

Durham knows himself to be Cherokee. Cherokee artists, curators, and writers Candice Byrd, Lynne Harlan, Luzene Hill, Ashley Holland, Brian K. Hudson, America Meredith, Pauline Prater, Yvonne N. Tiger, Kade Twist, and Cara Cowan Watts released a statement insisting that Durham is not because he is not enrolled in the Eastern Band of Cherokee Indians, the United Keetoowah Band of Cherokee Indians of Oklahoma, or the Cherokee Nation; does not provide proof of Cherokee ancestry; and is not affiliated with a recognized Cherokee community (Watts et al. 2017). Durham did not respond to their publication, a silent "no" to engage, perhaps because he has previously addressed his identity. In 1993, Durham stated that he is not a Cherokee or an Indian artist according to the then recent US legislation (1993, 23), the 1990 Indian Arts and Crafts Act, which establishes that people who exhibit art labeled Indian must be enrolled in or sanctioned by a recognized American Indian tribe. Durham did not relinquish his Cherokee identity, but maintained that it is not dependent on enrollment. People listed on the US Cherokee rolls were able to receive from the American government individual allotments of land carved out from reservations (Barker 2003). In a 1996 interview, Durham argues that allotment facilitated a shift from traditional forms of Cherokee sovereignty tied to relationship with kin in land toward private property and federally recognized Cherokee governments tied structurally to destructive US policies. In light of this assessment, Durham states that he does not recognize the authority of official Cherokee nations and their citizens to define his identity (Papastergiadis and Turney 1996, 31–38). He therefore offers no proof that he and his family were or are qualified to enroll, and no documented information about his heritage or upbringing.

Two signatories of the statement disavowing Durham, Cherokee Nation independent curator and writer Ashley Holland and Cherokee Nation artist and *First American Art Magazine* publishing editor America Meredith, followed up the statement with articles about Durham that address enrollment, heritage, and family (2017; 2017a, 2017b). Both writers note that enrollment has a fraught history but that today it establishes tribal self-determination and sovereignty as a bulwark against ongoing efforts to eradicate American Indians. Holland and Meredith also state that internet genealogical research shows that Durham has no Cherokee ancestors, and further point to the importance of living bonds among American Indians – that a "Native person's family remains a pivotal aspect of his or her identity and place in the community" (Holland 2017).

In a statement that addresses these issues, Los Angeles' Hammer Museum Senior Curator Anne Ellegood, curator of Durham's North American retrospective, observes that family names from both sides of the artist's family appear on two rolls used to establish Cherokee citizenship. She also notes that while Durham has not been claimed by an official Cherokee government, "there are many in the field of contemporary Indigenous art who believe Durham's claims of Cherokee ancestry," but that some are only comfortable supporting Durham privately because the controversy surrounding him is so heated (2017). Lyndon J. Linklater, Indigenous Relations Advisor at Saskatoon's Remai Modern, which exhibited the Durham retrospective in Canada, in a statement that honors those who do not accept Durham's claim to Cherokee identity, says that the museum is "also aware of those who support his identification as a Cherokee, a group that includes Indigenous people" (2018). Ellegood and Linklater note that Durham has a long history of work with and support from Native peoples.

When he lived in the US, Durham worked for indigenous rights in the American Indian Movement (AIM). He did so on the ground from 1973 during struggles for Native self-determination at Pine Ridge Reservation and in Indian survival schools, and from 1975 to 1979, as executive director of AIM's International Indian Treaty Council, its representative to the United Nations for Indians of

North and South America fighting for recognition as sovereign peoples (Stevens 2017, 289–90). Durham left AIM in 1979, believing that factionalism and government infiltration in the movement prevented it from working effectively for all American Indians (1980). During these efforts, which in and of themselves are no measure of Indian identity (Meredith 2017b), Durham labored with activists who are citizens of official Indian nations, who then and now find him Cherokee. One, who affirmed his recognition of Durham in a talk delivered during the artist's 2017–18 retrospective, is Comanche author and curator Paul Chaat Smith (2017). Smith worked with Durham in AIM and New York projects for underrepresented artists, and has written about Durham from the beginning of his career to the present.

I honor the positions of Cherokees and American Indians who do and do not accept Durham as Cherokee. I am not an American Indian and have learned a great deal about Indian identity through the discussion and debate about Durham. I see that Cherokee citizenship and Cherokee identity are both grounded in lived relationships among Cherokees who recognize one another through shared commitments to Cherokee kin, sovereignty, worldview, and lifeways. I also see that coalitions of American Indians from different nations are grounded in lived relationships among one another where recognition hinges on shared commitments to Indian kin, sovereignty, worldviews, and lifeways. Smith's discussion of Durham recounted their on-the-ground political work in AIM and the art world as forged through understanding of and trust in who they are as American Indians: Cherokee in one instance and Comanche in the other. I cannot say "no" to Durham's Cherokee identity when it is recognized by an American Indian, in this instance Comanche, who is recognized by and lives in relationship with fellow American Indians of many nations. Linklater's and Ellegood's statements about Durham's identity make evident that other Native people inhabit Smith's position.

Cherokee citizens and self-identified Cherokees in my area and stakeholders in the art world and academia have discussed with me their experience and understanding of Cherokee identity and Indian identity more broadly. I see that tribal citizenship girds Cherokees' and other Indians' self-determination: it establishes the identity and continuity of peoples who fight for their land and nourish their lifeways and wellbeing. I see that enrollment is difficult: for some, on political grounds and for others, it is hard to obtain. In the case of self-identified Cherokees, they may not be able to establish links between themselves and their last names listed on nineteenth- or early twentieth-century rolls. Alternatively, self-identified Cherokees may have no family members on rolls because they refused to enroll, were not counted, or chose to pass as whites to protect themselves from racism. Such families may have left no documents that mark Cherokee experience although they lived or live it. Their identities and those of their descendants are therefore fraught. I have encountered the latter scenario in the Cherokee homelands of South Carolina where I live and work. Conversation about Cherokee past, current, and future circumstances is beginning slowly but surely at Clemson University, where I teach. If a discussion of Cherokee identity here ensues, it will involve official Cherokees and those with Cherokee heritage, some of whom cannot prove this even though they have known or experience aspects of Cherokee life with non-enrolled family members. Such dialogues would surely entail disagreement, agreement, and uncertainty, but if they take place, they will open a space for participants to bring forth and take up histories, legacies, and ongoing conditions of colonization that affected and affect Cherokees in South Carolina and elsewhere.

Conflict may ensue, but that surrounding Durham's identity shows that however difficult, it has constructive dimensions. When Durham's retrospective traveled to the Minneapolis Walker Art Center, Sičangu Lakota artist Dyani White Hawk, Haudenosaunee (Seneca, Heron Clan), choreographer Rosy Simas, and Ojibwe (Turtle Mountain Band) poets and writers Heid E. Erdrich and Louise Erdrich met with museum officials, including now former Walker Director Olga Viso and retrospective curator Ellegood. Afterward, the Walker provided a disclaimer at the entrance of Durham's exhibition that stated that he is not a citizen of any of the three Cherokee nations and that some Cherokee artists and scholars reject his claim to Cherokee heritage (Regan 2017). Native peoples in the arts' efforts to have their voices on Durham heard were accompanied by their calls for the mainstream art world to embrace the artwork and expertise of Indian citizens. This had very important results. Curators and educators at museums that featured Durham's retrospective created with Native artists, curators, and scholars forums to discuss and debate issues of Indian identity and representation, and produced materials to educate people about Indian histories, current life, politics, art, and writing. All of these key resources are archived at the Hammer Museum, Walker Art Center, Whitney Museum of American Art, and Remai Modern websites.

Therefore, after community surrounding Durham's work broke down, some formed through exchanges that took up Indian circumstances and art. Many tensions remain, but I believe that shifts in perspective as well as unswerving commitment to positions are both important, for when people have the occasion to address and/ or perhaps test their convictions, all involved get a good sense of one another's politics, where coalitions can or cannot form, and how desired change might be effected. Durham's silent "no" to revisit challenges to his person frustrated and angered many; however, like the "no" of his critics, it helped shape settings where people thought through and acted upon their beliefs, measuring them alongside others, and determining where they stand.

With respect to place, Americans stand on American Indian, Native Hawaiian, and Native Alaskan homelands taken by British, European, and American colonizers, and claimed by the US today. Eighteenth- and nineteenth-century colonizers viewed Native land as property destined to yield profit through staples and manufactures, and Native people as impediments to such "progress" who must die, labor as slaves (Gallay 2002), or assimilate. This appetite for extraction and destruction fueled the plantation complex of the American South, business in the American North, and subsequent industries across the continent and in Hawai'i and Alaska. Established by white elites, these enterprises enriched a few at the expense of all Natives and their lands, and those made possible by slavery, did so on the backs of black slaves literally denied self-possession and forced to produce wealth for their abusers. Native homelands and enslaved persons were ground, as thing and verb, for white colonizers' inhuman practices of creating what they defined as "civilization" in North American and beyond (King 2014; Barker 2018). As History and Gender Studies scholar Maile Arvin (Kanaka Maoli), Native Feminist Methodologies scholar and educator Angie Morrill (Klamath), and Critical Race and Indigenous Studies scholar Eve Tuck (Unangax̂) state,

> The triad relationship among the industrious settler, the erased/ invisibilized Native, and the ownable and murderable slave is evident in the ways in which the United States continues to exploit Indigenous, black, and other peoples deemed "illegal" (or otherwise threatening and usurping) immigrants ....
>
> (2013, 12)

Examples from American histories and current conditions bear this out. After Emancipation, Chinese indentured labor provided "free" but cheap labor to build the US intercontinental railroad, which cut through Native territories and lives (Karuka 2019), and to work – along with Japanese contract laborers whose descendants were interred during World War II – corporate sugar plantations on land that once sustained Native Hawaiians (Maclennan 1997). Since the beginning of the twentieth century, Native Alaskan and Asian (many Filipino) cannery workers have lived and labored in the former's homelands in often inhuman conditions (Hinnershitz 2013), and Mexicans who worked in agriculture and other concerns, most of whom were US citizens, were forcibly expatriated from American states during the Depression (Little 2019) and fear deportation today (Spickard 2007). After the 2001 Patriot Act passed, which enables the US government to hold suspected "terrorists" without legal representation for unlimited time, approximately 1,000 Arab, South Asian, and Muslim men were imprisoned in undisclosed locations (Adams, Bell, and Griffin 2007).

These traumas and others embedded in past and current private, government, and corporate destruction of life and land affect the environment, livelihood, and wellbeing of many people – mostly poor – who today live on indigenous homelands claimed by America. Americans pay attention to what affects their standing and to those for whom and that for which they care, which sometimes includes people unlike themselves and sometimes, ravaged ecosystems. However, most of us do not realize or recognize that we occupy indigenous lands worked by slaves that are marked by past and current horrors, place the US government obtained by breaking treaties with Indian governments (Harjo 2014), overthrowing Hawai'i's monarchy (Silva 2004), and making Native Alaskans shareholders of their lands' surfaces, while companies gain access to subsurface resources (Tuck 2014).

After leaving AIM in 1979, Durham continued to critique and condemn Euro-American beliefs and practices such as these that abuse Native peoples and their homelands. He did so through art, essays, and poetry, and by helping to organize exhibitions that featured American Indian artwork. In his art, Durham criticized fetishized, institutionalized, and commodified representations of Indians and their creations. His 1985 *On Loan from the Museum of the American Indian* takes up drives to authenticate Indian artifacts: the installation displays a museum's "real" Indian goods that Durham made from natural elements associated with Native arts and fabricated items tied to American consumerism. His 1992 *Caliban Codex*, composed of drawings and small sculptures, examines racism at the core of colonization and its cultural representations: it shows Shakespeare's Caribbean Indian Caliban struggling to see and represent himself free from his master's monstrous projections. Durham's 1986 *Self-Portrait* assemblage explores a similar dynamic in contemporary stereotypes of Indians: the artist portrays himself as trophy-like, flayed red skin with crude face paint and synthetic braid, crisscrossed with his own handwritten, humanizing statements. The latter piece appeared in the 1993 Whitney Biennial, an exhibition both vilified and admired for showcasing underrepresented artists who address social injustice and its relationships to misrepresentations of minorities.

While in New York, and subsequently in Cuernavaca from 1987, Durham formed community with underrepresented artists, as he had when he first practiced art. In the 1960s, when he connected with other creators in Houston and then Austin, he performed in theater, wrote and read poems, and exhibited paintings and sculpture alongside politicized African American and Mexican American fellows. His work in Houston Theater was linked to community organizing, and his poetry and art grew through his friendship with Pulitzer Prize nominated African American poet Vivian Ayers Allen, who wrote of black women's challenges, developed education programs for disadvantaged youth, and supported underrepresented artists. In New York, from 1981 to 1983, Durham directed the Foundation for the Community of Artists, which provided fellow creators with healthcare, and produced a newsletter that gave emerging writers a voice. In 1982, he appeared in his first group show, Juan Sánchez's *Beyond Aesthetics: Art of Necessity by Artists of Conscience*, and first exhibited work at Joe Overstreet, Corrine Jennings, and Samuel C. Floyd's Kenkeleba Gallery, devoted to artists of color. In 1984, Durham took part in the multi-venue program *ARTISTS CALL against US Intervention in Central America* and the exhibition *Call and Response: Art on Central America*. In 1986 and 1987, he co-curated two group shows of art by American Indians with Jean Fisher, who included him in a 1988 London show, his first in Europe (Stevens 2017, 290–93). While in the US and Mexico, Durham produced his artwork, curating, essays, performance, and poetry critical of colonization alongside and in solidarity with art world activists who tackled other forms of abuse. Attentive to human cruelty in all its manifestations, he addressed those particular to the places he worked, and the circumstances he lived or learned of from others who shared their experiences with him. Therefore, when Durham left North America for Europe in 1994 to pursue projects he was invited to undertake there, he took up the Western exceptionalism that birthed colonization and other terrible iniquities (Horton 2017, 49) in the contexts of how they inform and can intensify conditions at specific European sites. Durham remains in Europe, which he often refers to as Eurasia both to make clear the interwoven histories and current realities that make up this entire continent, and to point to the exclusionary logic of referring to European nations outside the British Isles as "the continent." In the European places Durham is asked to exhibit, he investigates some of the material and political conditions that break down beings, alongside other arrangements that can build them up.

The title for this book, *Jimmie Durham, Europe, and the Art of Relations*, is the frame for my discussion of four projects he completed recently in Europe that address some of its particulars: his 2005 *Something… Perhaps a Fugue or an Elegy*, 2016 and ongoing Neapolitan *presepi*, 2018 *The Middle Earth* with Maria Thereza Alves, and 2017 *God's Children, God's Poems*. I ground the terms art and relations, and how they can coordinate in Durham's work, in contexts of being and knowing in the Anthropocene, our age when humans likely will not repair the damage we have done to earth. As I examine and find meanings in Durham's projects, I consider how his materials through processes and arrangements open out to subjectivities in communities and polities of places. I argue that the affective and cognitive dimensions of his work situate viewers in relations of disconnection and connection as occasions to reflect on what constitutes value, and how our values and those of others operate to draw being together and apart. I think through these possibilities by attending to how I see "and" as well as "with" arise in Durham's projects more so than "not" and "against." With *Something… Perhaps a Fugue or an Elegy*, I do so where arts take up individual and collective existential concerns; with his *presepi* where faith impacts community; with *The Middle Earth* with Maria Thereza Alves where humanity and inhumanity wrestle; and with *God's Children, God's Poems* where animal kin address how death in life does and does not burgeon. I see these projects as specific, small art worlds whereby the art of relations offers

> a basis from which to claim that other worlds are not a utopian horizon, but part of lived reality – albeit in partial, fragmentary and incipient forms. Such examples make it possible to see certain kinds of micro-struggles in relation to each other and in relation to macro-scale change.
>
> (McNevin 2020)

I believe that the Durham projects I examine elicit deep thinking about what and who are cast aside or brought together in Europe and its representations, what might happen when the latter occurs, and what such connections suggest in broader contexts of being together today. I think that every opportunity to explore ideas about and experiences of community in place is especially crucial now. Sweeping migrations, mass extinctions, and horrible disease brought on by war, economic collapse, and environmental degradation accompany ongoing colonization and virulently nationalistic policies that crush efforts to protect and nourish who and what suffer abuse. Artists freed from the worst of these circumstances can provide illuminating ways to take up how flourishing does and does not occur today. I believe that Durham's *Something... Perhaps a Fugue or an Elegy, presepi, The Middle Earth* with Maria Thereza Alves, and *God's Children, God's Poems* give those of us fortunate enough to explore art important opportunities to think critically about our situated relations with others and what these relations may make possible.

References

Adams, Maurianne, Lee Anne Bell, and Pat Griffin, eds. 2007. "History of Racism and Immigration Time Line Key Events in the Struggle for Racial Equality in the United States." In *Teaching for Diversity and Social Justice*, 2nd ed. New York: Routledge. https://doi.org/10.4324/9780203940822.

Arvin, Maile, Eve Tuck, and Angie Morrill. 2013. "Decolonizing Feminism: Challenging Connections between Settler Colonialism and Heteropatriarchy." *Feminist Formations* 25, no. 1 (Spring): 8–34. https://doi.org/10.1353/ff.2013.0006.

Barker, Joanne. 2003. "Indian TM U.S.A." *Wicazo Sa Review* 18, no. 1: 25–79. https://doi.org/10.1353/wic.2003.0002.

———. 2018. "Decolonizing the Mind." *Rethinking Marxism* 30, no. 2: 208–31. https://doi.org/10.1080/08935696.2018.1502308 209.

Durham, Jimmie. 1980. "An Open Letter on Recent Developments in the American Indian Movement/International Indian Treaty Council." In *A Certain Lack of Coherence*, edited by Jean Fisher, 46–56. London: Kala Press, 1993.

———. 1993. "Letter to the Editor." *Art in America* 81, no. 7 (July): 23.

———. 2014. "Is This Interesting?" *Mousse Contemporary Art Magazine* 42 (February–March): 194–95.

———. 2017. "Europe." In *God's Children, God's Poems*, edited by Heike Munder, 11–13. Zurich: Migros Museum für Gegenwartskunst and JRP|Ringier.

Ellegood, Anne. 2017. "Curator Anne Ellegood on Understanding the Complexities of Jimmie Durham's Native Identity." *Artnet*, August 2, 2017. https://news.artnet.com/opinion/anne-ellegood-jimmie-durham-1033907.

Gallay, Alan. 2002. *The Indian Slave Trade: The Rise of the English Empire in the American South, 1670–1717.* New Haven, CT: Yale University Press. https://doi.org/10.1353/cal.2016.0135.

Harjo, Suzan Shown, ed. 2014. *Nation to Nation: Treaties between the United States & American Indian Nations.* Washington, DC: National Museum of the American Indian in association with Smithsonian Books.

Hinnershitz, Stephanie. 2013. "'We Ask Not for Mercy, but for Justice': The Cannery Workers and Farm Laborers' Union and Filipino Civil Rights in the United States, 1927–1937." *Journal of Social History* 47, no. 1 (Fall): 132–52.

Holland, Ashley. 2017. "Issues & Commentary: The Artist Formerly Known as Cherokee." *Art in America*, August 15, 2017. https://www.artnews.com/art-in-america/features/issues-commentary-the-artist-formerly-known-as-cherokee-63284/.

Horton, Jessica L. 2017. *Art for an Undivided Earth: The American Indian Movement Generation.* Durham, NC and London: Duke University Press. https://doi.org/10.1215/9780822372790.

Karuka, Manu. 2019. *Empire's Tracks: Indigenous Nations, Chinese Workers, and the Transcontinental Railroad.* Oakland: University of California Press. https://doi.org/10.1525/9780520969056.

King, Tiffany. 2014. "Labor's Aphasia: Toward Antiblackness as Constitutive to Settler Colonialism." *Decolonization: Indigeneity, Education & Society*, June 10, 2014. https://decolonization.wordpress.com/2014/06/10/labors-aphasia-toward-antiblackness-as-constitutive-to-settler-colonialism/#_ftnref4.

Linklater, Lyndon J. 2018. "Jimmie Durham: At the Center of the World." Remai Modern website, March 15, 2018. https://remaimodern.org/field/read/jimmie-durham-at-the-center-of-the-world-lyndon-j-linklater-indigenous-relations-advisor.

Little, Becky. 2019. "The U.S. Deported a Million of Its Own Citizens to Mexico during the Great Depression." *History*, July 12, 2019. https://www.history.com/news/great-depression-repatriation-drives-mexico-deportation.

Maclennan, Carol A. 1997. "Hawai'i Turns to Sugar: The Rise of Plantation Centers, 1860–1880." *The Hawaiian Journal of History* 31: 97–125.

McNevin, Anne. 2020. "Borders, Migration, and the Urgency of Imagination." *Vacarme*, 89/cahier, February 16, 2020. https://vacarme.org/article3308.html.

Meredith, America. 2017a. "Why It Matters That Jimmie Durham Is Not a Cherokee." *Artnet*, July 7, 2017. https://news.artnet.com/opinion/jimmie-durham-america-meredith-1014164.

———. 2017b. "Issues & Commentary: Ethnic Fraud and Art." *Art in America*, August 15, 2017. https://www.artnews.com/art-in-america/features/issues-commentary-ethnic-fraud-and-art-63285/.

Papastergiadis, Nikos, and Laura Turney. 1996. *On Becoming Authentic: Interview with Jimmie Durham*. Cambridge, UK: Prickly Pear Press.

Regan, Sheila. 2017. "Jimmie Durham Retrospective Reignites Debate over His Claim of Native Ancestry." *Hyperallergic*, June 28, 2017. https://hyperallergic.com/387970/jimmie-durham-retrospective-reignites-debate-over-his-claim-of-native-ancestry/.

Silva, Noenoe K. 2004. *Aloha Betrayed: Native Hawaiian Resistance to American Colonialism*. Durham, NC and London: Duke University Press. https://doi.org/10.1215/9780822386223.

Smith, Paul Chaat. 2017. "The Most American Thing Ever Is in Fact American Indians." Walker Art Center website, August 31, 2017. https://walkerart.org/magazine/paul-chaat-smith-jimmie-durham-americans-nmai-smithsonian.

Spickard, Paul. 2007. *Almost All Aliens: Immigration, Race, and Colonialism in American History and Identity*. New York: Routledge, 2007. https://doi.org/10.1086/ahr.116.5.1478.

Stevens, MacKenzie. 2017. "Selected Chronology." In *Jimmie Durham: At the Center of the World*, edited by Anne Ellegood, 288–303. Los Angeles, CA: Hammer Museum; Munich and New York: Prestel.

Tuck, Eve. 2014. "ANCSA as x-mark: Surface and Subsurface Claims of the Alaska Native Claims Settlement Act." *Alaska Native Studies* 1, no. 1: 240–72.

Watts, Cara Cowan et al. 2017. "Dear Unsuspecting Public, Jimmie Durham Is a Trickster." *Indian Country Today*, June 26, 2017. https://newsmaven.io/indiancountrytoday/archive/dear-unsuspecting-public-jimmie-durham-is-a-trickster-Rk7_oZ6TPkmIlQLNJN-gPw.

1   Art Matters

*Something ... Perhaps a
Fugue or an Elegy,* 2005

Durham's 15. May we 2005 *Something ... Perhaps a Fugue or an
Elegy* is a very large assemblage composed of many broken objects,
including outmoded communication devices, varied building materials, disjointed animal bones, and two Classical plaster heads.
Something debuted at the 2005 Venice Biennale, the world's pre-
mier contemporary art fair dedicated to visual art, architecture,
film, dance, music, and theater, an event that involves a great deal
of international press, hundreds of top art world figures, and tens
of thousands of visitors over six months. *Something ... Perhaps a
Fugue or an Elegy*'s title told its large audience that it was looking
at visual art as music and poetry at the very site in Europe where all
arts are resoundingly celebrated today.

In his review of the 2005 Venice Biennale, critic Hal Foster argues that ethnopoetic bricolage is a major feature of the fair, and a
practice that Durham among others initiated. Ethnopoetics speaks
to the work of poets and other creators who explore cultural traditions little known or undervalued in the West (Rothenberg 1993),
and bricolage in art describes the combination of materials at hand
evident in collage and assemblage. Foster maintains that ethnopoetic bricolage at the 2005 Biennale extends that made by modern
European artists, who "caught up in an earlier moment of the dia-
lectic of technological transformation and cultural confrontation,
of 'futurism' and 'primitivism,'" sought responses to the effects of
modernization. For Foster, the "contrast and/or combination of ad-
vanced and archaic means, of new and outmoded media" in contemporary ethnopoetic bricolage engages "the forces of media, market,
and empire" naturalized as "globalization" (2005).

With these terms, Foster evokes today's neoliberal capitalism,
which is propelled chiefly by supranational extractive, retail, ser-
vice, and manufacturing industries. These businesses fuel climate
change, regularly ruin place, often ill-use workers, and funnel

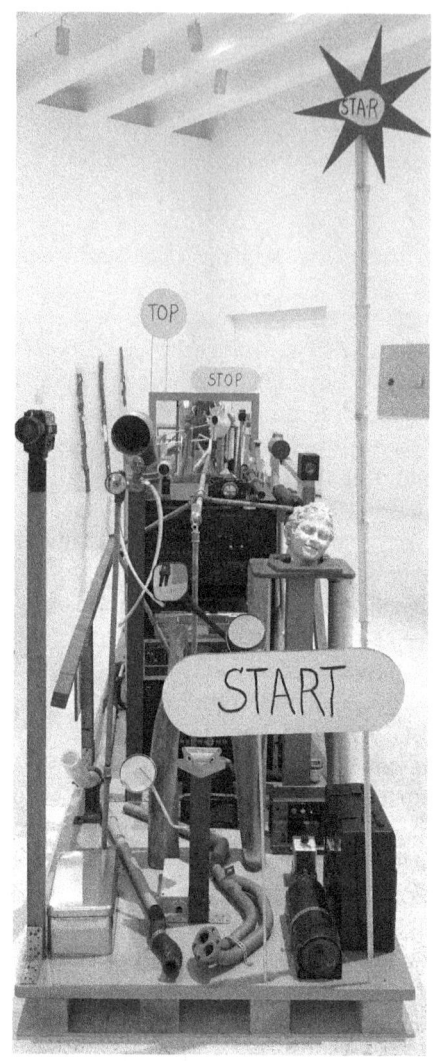

Figure 1.1 Jimmie Durham, *Something … Perhaps a Fugue or an Elegy*, 2005, cameras, television, VHS player, amplifier, tripod, steel pipes, hardware, PVC pipes, plastic, rope, acrylic paint, pine, seashell, brass heads, cast marble-dust head, oak box, glass bottle, wood furniture parts, tree branches, tire, mirrors, metal lock, metal chains, lights, wires, plywood pallets, armadillo shell, cow skull and bones, ink on paper, 71 × 275 ½ × 63 in. (180 × 600 × 100 cm) – Courtesy Collezione Morra Greco, Napoli (view, Walker Art Center, Minneapolis, 2017).

wealth through global networks to individual, corporate, and government power brokers. Product brands and ads delivered through digital, broadcast, and print media veil this exploitation and invite consumers to buy into its orbit by purchasing goods ultimately discarded.

Viewed in Foster's framework, *Something ... Perhaps a Fugue or an Elegy* sits squarely within literal and figurative investments in global communication and consumption in a city and fair embedded in both. Venice is a former maritime republic established at cultural crossroads that ran powerful worldwide trade networks from the tenth through mid-fifteenth centuries. Today, it is a UNESCO World Heritage site filled with masterpieces of art and architecture from Byzantine times to the present, a city that inspired and continues to inspire poetic and musical as well as visual creation. Venice's cultural riches, including those on view during the Venice Biennale, rest precariously amid canals within a lagoon, and the litter and carbon footprint of millions of tourists burden a place already sinking as seas rise with climate change. Thus at its debut, *Something ... Perhaps a Fugue or an Elegy* was an encounter with art in global networks of commerce and influence layered within earlier histories of the same.

In the statement for the Venice Biennale international exhibition she organized, which included *Something ... Perhaps a Fugue or an Elegy*, curator Rosa Martínez evokes travel and networks to describe her vision of contemporary art and its place in the world:

> ... the exhibition *Always a Little Further* is an essay presenting artists and aesthetic trends relevant at the beginning of the third millennium. A visit to the [Biennale] Arsenale proposes a fragmentary trip, a subjective and passionate dramatization to discover the zones of light and dark in our convulsed world. This journey intends to draw the most significant lines in contemporary artistic production and to show that art still holds a promise for those who want to embark on the sort of voyage that made [philosopher Gilles] Deleuze take [writer Marcel] Proust's motto: the real dreamer is the one who goes out to try to verify something.
>
> (2005)

In vivid, poetic language, Martínez proposes an experience of discovery linked to voyage – an image that resonates with Venice as a maritime art capital – asking viewers to imagine themselves traveling with her as she follows artists who search for light amid the world's darkness. In her framework, a powerful romantic trope, Martínez points to how art often engages individuals in a search for meaning.

Durham's *Something … Perhaps a Fugue or an Elegy* resonates with Martínez's ideas about art and fraught individual questioning in relation to Foster's ideas about the structural conditions of contemporary art and life as globalization. The assemblage does so in the context of how art in Europe is a key site – as a privileged, influential practice positioned to address a wide art audience – of expansive meditation on conditions that concern many. In this instance, loss and gain as well as ruin and creation in people's experiences of culture, politics, and mortality.

Like most of Durham's work, *Something … Perhaps a Fugue or an Elegy* is made from a vast collection of materials in all sizes that the artist encounters where he works and to which he adds constantly. Durham fills his studios and work sites with sticks and stones he comes across in wooded areas; broken glass and crushed paper he discovers in city streets; outdated mechanisms and personal goods he purchases at flea markets; car parts and furniture scraps he gathers at junkyards; old clothing and household goods he acquires at thrift shops; bits and pieces of building supplies he buys at hardware stores; and animal remains he finds or receives wherever he goes. Durham makes his art with what many people deem trash: whether old or new, natural or manufactured, intact or damaged, everything he employs is seemingly unremarkable, or even unattractive. When I visited his Berlin studio in 2017 and his Naples studio in 2018, I encountered the largest collections of diverse materials I have ever seen. Durham seemed to know where and how he had acquired each item in his workspaces, and where to find materials he sought for a particular project, whether they sprawled on the floor, occupied shelves, nestled in boxes, or hid within piles on his worktable. It was clear to me that he has intimate relationships with treasured things.

Durham keeps company with many other artists committed to humble and sometimes unappealing materials. Foster's review of the 2005 Venice Biennale reminds readers that the practices and results of bricolage are longstanding. Modern artists used bits and pieces of everyday life in their projects to reconfigure art's relationships to traditional aesthetics, representational strategies, and social circumstances. Among standouts are Pablo Picasso's and Georges Braque's Cubist collages of the 1910s that challenge notions of the "real" in art; Marcel Duchamp's readymades from the same decade forward that spurn "retinal" painting in favor of conceptual art; and Hannah Höch's photomontages that critique normative representations of women. Contemporary collage and assemblage also involve art's material and social conditions. Well-known examples span the 1950s to the present and include Richard Hamilton's Pop collages that address rampant consumption; Robert Rauschenberg's Neo Dada combines that critique late Modernism's insular abstraction; and Betye Saar's bricolage that attacks American racism. Bricolage was and remains an important medium for artists to expand art's materials, processes, and concepts (Seitz 1961; Dezeuze 2008; Kelly 2008), and is an approach to making art that Durham often favors.

Durham suggests why in his 1992 essay "On the Edge of Town," which speaks of the things, procedures, and ideas he assembles. In this text, he describes the borderland between built and "undeveloped" environments as a dump. Wild animals and the city's detritus occupy this place, and its human cast-offs – "families of African-Americans and displaced Indians" – make use of thrown-away objects to sustain themselves. A jumble of broken products, pieces of wood, bones, wild flowers, and "magic stones," Durham's dump is the site where he encounters materials that knit him together with being sentient and otherwise, and with which he produces art. He is not apart from the stuff of the world, no matter how ugly, but a part of it in ways both critical and constructive that help him create (251).

This condition underpins his 1997 *Public Monument for the Birthday of Rome*, an outdoor installation "on the edge of town" that takes up Rome as a representation and reality. The piece consists of a large garbage mound sited with a view of St. Peter's Basilica, the seat of the Roman Catholic Church both uplifting and oppressive; embodiment of Renaissance architecture and art both innovative and endlessly copied; and symbol of Rome's civic legacies both republican and imperial. Two photographs document *Public Monument for the Birthday of Rome*: one shows Durham sprawled on top of the work's front portion, and the other pictures him standing alongside the installation with St. Peter's far in the background. These images suggest that Durham is not removed from his anti-monument to the "eternal city" of Western civilization, the Rome that dominated and continues to impact much of the world through models of governance, religion, architecture, and art. As an artist then working in Rome, Durham is in and alongside the

city's real and metaphorical wreckage and its actual and romanti-
cized images even as he contrasts them. *Public Monument for the
Birthday of Rome* literally and figuratively shows viewers what we
are not meant to see of the city's past and present: that ruin and
trash accompany invention and sustenance in Rome's culture and/
as politics.

Like the *Public Monument for the Birthday of Rome, Something …
Perhaps a Fugue or an Elegy* rejects idealization and explores lived
destruction and creation by using rubbish as well as associations
that attend forms of European art. *Something … Perhaps a Fugue
or an Elegy* takes up the musical fugue and poetic elegy without
scrubbing the latter, which often sanitizes while ennobling a dead
person's life. The assemblage also brings junk into the refined space
of the Venice Biennale, detritus like that in trash piles increasingly
visible in Venice and all over the world. The piece shows that art can
arise from and address any material, no matter how unwelcome:
indeed that death, the stuff of being we regularly push aside, exists amidst everything. *Something … Perhaps a Fugue or an Elegy*
points to creation and destruction and humans' part in both, for
better or worse. Large in scale, commanding in space, dense in
construction, and structured in form, the assemblage's conditions
embody the weight and power of making. However, *Something …
Perhaps a Fugue or an Elegy*'s elements, such as machine components, animal remains, building materials, and Classical art elements, are fragments affected by time arranged in a manner that
suggests they not only extend, but also have exhausted or exceeded
use to become waste.

This condition whereby something made transforms into something else less solid aligns the assemblage with the European music
and poetry of its title. Viewers are reminded that its creators use
material items – notes in music, words in poetry, and things in art –
to produce what seems substantial, but which ultimately melts into
air. Shakespeare turned this phrase to describe illusions, and Marx
adapted it to characterize capitalism (Percy 2011). Durham evokes
it to meditate on the aesthetic and political dimensions of invention
and ruin, and how both can be experienced. *Something … Perhaps
a Fugue or an Elegy* suggests that things produced and consumed
for pleasure and power in Europe – and the idea and experience
of the Western world it spawned – may or may not endure, prized
as the best of culture, or discarded into heaps of broken junk. The
assemblage asks those who view contemporary art to reflect on the
promising and problematic ways we make with and are unmade by

the stuff of our world, a timely request when the piece was created, and one that becomes increasingly urgent as the 2000s unfold further into the Anthropocene.

Components and Composition

Something ... Perhaps a Fugue or an Elegy is a large, freestanding sculpture on a slightly raised platform with a stated orientation: Durham labeled one end "START" and the other "STOP." When I viewed *Something ... Perhaps a Fugue or an Elegy* at the Hammer Museum and Walker Art Center during Durham's 2017–18 North American retrospective, I noted that museum visitors invariably circumambulated the assemblage so as to experience the piece from "START" and "STOP" and back again. I did this too, and beginning with "START," I saw a host of objects that faced me directly such as projecting mirrors, open pipes, trained camera lenses, a plaster head of Pan, and the aimed barrel of a rifle (see Figure 1.1). The latter underscores aggression in what looks like a confrontation with literal destruction in consumption and waste, although a small wood figure with round eyes at the front of the assemblage lightens the mood. This little entity compounds the creaturely dimension of *Something ... Perhaps a Fugue or an Elegy*'s parts: nearby pipes look like snakes for example, a resemblance made concrete by linked tubular components that include a sculpted snake body.

Encouraged to move toward "STOP" by snaking interconnected tubes and rhythmically placed rectangular items, I walked forward and encountered objects that evoke various senses, states, and ideas. A television emphasizes vision already accentuated with cameras and mirrors, and the sound associated with TV is evident in a radio and amplifier; that all are broken suggests failed communication. A tripod conjures balance also conveyed by a shell poised atop a pipe, and self-reflection signifies not only through images I saw of myself in mirrors scattered amid *Something ... Perhaps a Fugue or an Elegy*, but also because a plaster head of a putto faces a large mirror at the "STOP" end of the work. An arrow instantiates movement also evident in a tire, and several closed containers as well as a locked box embody inaccessibility. All of these parts communicate immanence and intangibility within and across one another, and called toward my moving body and processing mind while also indexing Durham's corporeal and intellectual work, and connecting me with it. When I arrived at "STOP," I encountered a cow skull and bones, with two of the latter bracketing the word "DEATH" – seemingly suspending finality. In order to read "DEATH" right way up, I had to face the beginning of the piece. Absence and presence, and my relationships to both, led me in different physical and cognitive directions as I circumambulated *Something … Perhaps a Fugue or an Elegy.*

These courted shifts convey the sense of give and take characteristic of dialogue and performance, much as conversation is conducted, music is played, and poetry is read. *Something … Perhaps a Fugue or an Elegy*'s elements, like notes and words, "speak" with one another through connections, breaks, absences, clusters, and accretions, and do so in a six-part armature that recalls the fugue's music staff and the elegy's poetry stanza. In the fugue, a European Baroque musical

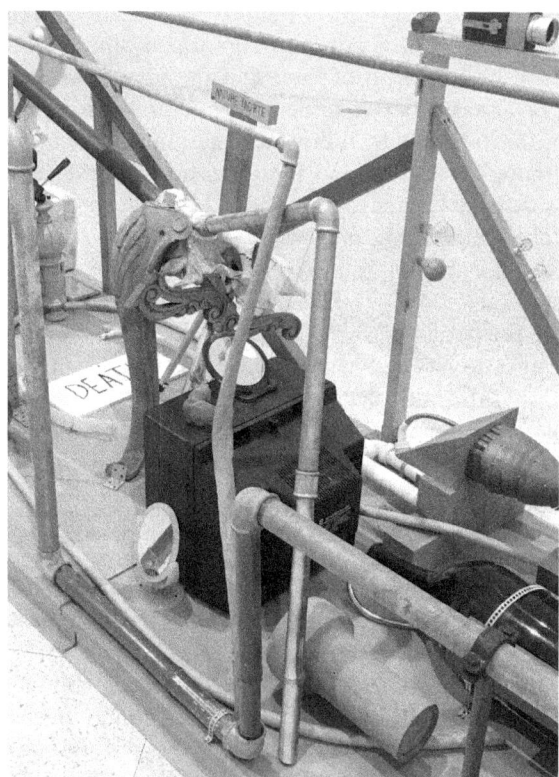

Figure 1.2 Jimmie Durham, *Something … Perhaps a Fugue or an Elegy*, detail of back end looking forward (view, Walker Art Center, Minneapolis, 2017).

form, two or more instrumental voices call and respond in set and often elaborate patterns of reflection and inversion, a rich auditory dynamic that parallels *Something … Perhaps a Fugue or an Elegy*'s complex visual strategies. A panel toward the back of the piece makes this especially clear: it contains rows of texts in different European languages that mean similar things. Voice also echoes and transforms in the elegy, a poem of mourning begun in Classical Greece that evolved from music to language as a sad tribute to a dead figure, or sorrowful reflection on mortality that ends in consolation (Hirsch 2014). *Something … Perhaps a Fugue or an Elegy* performs an equally layered reflection on death in life and culture. A beautifully carved chair leg frames and supports the cow skull in the assemblage, holding the death head aloft and helping it extend beyond itself through an attached network of elements that meet up with other parts. Further, the plaster heads of Pan and a putto face viewers and a mirror, respectively, suggesting the importance of seeing death in and perhaps the death of Classical culture. Separate-while-connected presence and absence diverge from and build upon one another as material arrangement in the assemblage, as they do in the fugue and elegy, now traditional Western art forms. First exhibited in Europe's most famous arts biennial, located in a European city of art dying through overexposure and climate change, *Something … Perhaps a Fugue or an Elegy* is a nuanced, situated meditation on European arts of life and death.

While Durham's assemblage draws its audience's attention to how its structure bears some relation to making in European music and poetry in the context of loss in life and culture, the brute "thingness" of the artwork's components keeps us close to thoughts about the stuff with which people live. The skull and bones, broken machine parts, and decapitated plaster heads not only invite meditation on demise, but also on the things humans consume and throw away. The cow's head and bones remind viewers that people chop animals into pieces that those of us who eat meat literally consume alongside parts we discard. The broken goods such as the TV and amplifier remind observers that when we no longer use our products, we toss them aside to deteriorate further in dumps. *Something … Perhaps a Fugue or an Elegy* represents not only a sort of contemporary decline in civilization, but also potential ruin of empire – made concrete with the Classical plaster heads – by showing that global capitalism's physical delivery systems, media mechanisms and consumer goods, can break down and fail to serve their users.

However, the assemblage's powerful indictment of consumption and its effects is offset by its potent tribute to the material of art – how it can be rooted in things that are awful *and* built into something that sustains. Durham reinforces the latter condition through his liberal use of actual building materials in *Something ... Perhaps a Fugue or an Elegy*. Pipes and pieces of wood form the artwork's armature and link the assemblage's components together in rhythmic unfolding through space, much like the fugue's and elegy's components move through structures on the page and in the air.

Something ... Perhaps a Fugue or an Elegy is a sort of puzzle about art and life: it asks its audience to think about how stuff falls apart and comes together, why we value some things and not others, and what makes different art forms similar and disparate. The assemblage addresses the problems with and promise of Europe's cultural and social formations, tying their materials, conditions, and arrangements to existential considerations personal and individual, as well as political and collective.

Means and Ends

Literary critic and Palestinian activist Edward Said, poet Ann Lauterbach, and feminist art historian Linda Nochlin analyze how European music's, poetry's, and visual art's material and compositional relations and dynamics can speak of and back to historical and current socio-political realities. They also argue that the arts they take up can model something critical, uplifting, and empowering from and in a world torn by oppressive Western praxis. Said, Lauterbach, and Nochlin suggest that this happens when musicians, poets, artists, and writers subvert controlled and controlling artistic structures and their valences by ushering new, different, and connected material elements into such forms. The three writers look closely at how experimental Western creators use individual parts – notes, words, visual elements – to assemble compositions that thwart stated or implied directives through art. Broadly, their focus on pieces marshaled in disruptive arrangements reflects critical postmodern theory indebted to philosopher François Lyotard's critique of totalizing Western "metanarratives" that foreclose non-normative ideas and experiences.

Said is best known for his study of Orientalism, which shows how Western political and cultural devices work to render peoples of the Middle East, North Africa, and Asia exotic and/or savage "Others" as an alibi for colonization and containment (1978). In his work with music as a pianist, collaborator, and critic, Said considers the positive dimensions of cultural and political interactions. He did so concretely when he created with Israeli conductor Daniel Barenboim the West-Eastern Divan Orchestra through which musicians work across political divides to give voice to joyful rather than hateful assemblage. When he writes of music in the European tradition, Said considers how some compositions themselves shepherd divergent instrumental voices into restraining arrangements in order to unbind them. He sees this in work by composers such as Wolfgang Mozart, Richard Strauss, and Glen Gould that infuse lush counterpoint and strategic digression into fixed linearity. For Said, the resulting rich polyphony and layered temporality produce an aesthetic model for how social interaction might challenge authoritative structures and narratives (Wood 2004; Fry 2008). Speaking of Gould on Strauss, Said addresses his own understanding of what the latter produced:

> ... it is, I believe, radically, beautifully elaborative, music whose pleasures and discoveries are premised upon letting go, upon not asserting a central authorizing identity, upon enlarging the community of hearers and players beyond the time taken, beyond the extremely concentrated duration provided by the performance occasion. In this perspective afforded by such a work as *Metamorphosen*, music thus becomes an art not primarily or exclusively about authorial power and social authority, but a mode for thinking through or thinking with the integral variety of human cultural practices, generously, noncoercively, and yes, in a utopian cast, if by utopian we mean worldly, possible, attainable, knowable.
>
> (Wood 2004, 148)

Lauterbach practices and writes about a similar dynamic in form that poetry of the West can take. In many of her poems, she adds quotes from past and present European creators, producing conversation among different voices to undercut a single, authorial voice. For example, her 2018 *Spell* contains poems in dialogue with work by the Roman poets Lucretius and Ovid, as well as with Giuseppe Verdi's opera *Otello*, based on William Shakespeare's play *Othello*. Relationships among parts in all of her poetic assemblages trace constellations of diverging paths that put pressure on stable Western aesthetic and social norms. Lauterbach embeds her project within poetry itself, which she argues brings together bits and pieces of the world to fashion values through "new ideas of coherence, where boundaries are malleable and permeable, so that inclusion and exclusion are in unstable flux" (2008, "Use This Word in a Sentence") against social proscription. She maintains that

> Art serves no practical purpose, but to engage with it fully is to acknowledge the (pleasurable, if often difficult) consequences of choice at the crux of human agency. I want to suggest that artworks can disrupt the degradation of choice as the site of, and synonymous with, commodification (consumer preference) and (re)align it with the rewards of independent determinations of value – processes of aesthetic discernment and critique seen as part of a continuum across individual, social, political terrain (Introduction).

While the assemblage of parts has a utopian cast in Said's and Lauterbach's meditations on music and poetry in the European tradition, this does not seem to be the case for art historian Linda Nochlin's reflections on Western art – at least initially. In her discussion of how European and American modern and contemporary artists represent body parts and compose with them, Nochlin draws readers' attention to material with a disturbing, visceral charge. Further, Nochlin concerns herself with how the form and content of parts and assemblages in experimental Western visual art can signal dissolution as ruin and embody assertion of control.

Nochlin reminds her readers that idealized, classically inspired bodies were key components of Western art prior to and several decades after the French Revolution, driving visual narratives about elites' power. She maintains that as traditional political and social bodies broke down in Europe, so too did traditionally represented human bodies – toward different ends and with different effects. In modern European art, she argues that body fragments signal mourning for the lost "whole" of heroic Classicism; represent bodies broken in political turmoil; function as metaphors for capitalist and bourgeois disconnection; suggest the contingency of everyday life; or embody an artist's drive to manage anxiety through the fetish. Nochlin states that this impetus to fragment the body in modern art is countered by the *Gesamtkunstwerk* (the total work of art as a design for living), in a dialectical move toward totalization. She defines this will to control as a "struggle to overcome the disintegrative effects – social, psychic, political – inscribed in modern, particularly modern urban, experience, by hypostatizing them within a higher unity" (1995, 53). Whether broken down or built up, Nochlin views the modern art compositions she studies as exemplars of fraught rather than freeing relations. She seems less sanguine than Said and Lauterbach when it comes to interrelationships between art and life in the West.

However, when Nochlin turns her attention to critical postmodern art, she sees a dynamic at work similar to those Said and Lauterbach find in the Western music and poetry they favor. Nochlin argues that contemporary artists like Louise Bourgeois, Cindy Sherman, and Robert Mapplethorpe arrange body parts into compositions that challenge oppressive constructs, especially those that ascribe inherent authority to the white, heterosexual male body. She maintains that the "body-in-pieces" becomes the logic of Western postmodern art indebted to Europe that breaks down totalizing narratives in the body politic (55). Here, Nochlin's reflections on parts in assemblage open out onto the possibilities for critical, constructive social relations that Said and Lauterbach believe some forms of European music and poetry model.

Nochlin's work reassembles art history by shedding light on the work of artists absent from the art historical canon, which charts the heroic achievements of normative European and Euro-American male artists. Among other white, straight feminist critics and artists allied with those of color and varied sexual identities and orientations, Nochlin pursues different and multiple ways of composing critical and expansive definitions and experiences of art. She describes her writing as a combinatory practice against the grain of established measures:

> I believe that traditional, strictly defined methodology is very reductive, because it assumes the universality of a single perspective. Writing history "Otherly," is, once again, a dialectic process. As I formulate the issue, the methodology, so to speak, grows partly out of it, and that's the notion of "bricolage," a kind of back-and-forth between problematizing the issue and the theoretical apparatus of approaching the issue. Such a methodology is always on the move, it shifts all the time, ...
>
> (2006)

Something ... Perhaps a Fugue or an Elegy is bricolage as Nochlin conceives it, Said hails it, Lauterbach practices it, and what all three hope for it. Broken parts in Durham's bricolage signal broken European art traditions and social conditions, but assembled in critical *and* hopeful ways, they suggest the making of new arrangements that are not. *Something ... Perhaps a Fugue or an Elegy* brings detritus, different European art forms, varied references, and separate directional orientations into relation with one another as the freeing polyphony Said and Lauterbach encourage in music and poetry, as well as the critical powers and agency Said, Lauterbach, and Nochlin find and model in arts of assemblage.

Death and Melancholy Reconsidered

Like Durham's installation the *Public Monument to the Birthday of Rome* and essay "On the Edge of Town," *Something … Perhaps a Fugue or an Elegy* insists that detritus has continued use – that there is something to be made, both literally and figuratively – from what we reject. However, a tall sign that Durham planted at the back end of the assemblage orients viewers toward unmaking, specifically, our own undoing. The sign paraphrases sad words from José Saramago's novel *The Year of the Death of Ricardo Reis*: "We worry, and are full of anxiety. We think the world will demand an explanation. But in fact the world has already moved on, and has forgotten us" (Saramago 1991, 78).

These statements establish a somber mood and reflect a melancholic disposition, a felt attitude typically characterized by immobilizing, depressed contemplation. Albrecht Dürer's well-known 1514 engraving *Melencholia I* portrays this state and links it to art: personified melancholy sits lost in unhappy reflection surrounded by her abandoned artists' tools. Art is stalled: its agents, elements, processes, and effects remain unassembled and dead to creation. This twining of art and death is inescapable in *Something … Perhaps a Fugue or an Elegy*. In addition to its allusion to the elegy, and its use of detritus including bones, the assemblage also points to death in and of art: it contains not only two plaster heads with Classical referents, but also a photo of the Greek ca. 500–490 BCE dying warrior sculpture from the Temple of Aphaia's west pediment. As with *Public Monument for the Birthday of Rome*, viewers are encouraged to consider whether ruin amidst Classical empire and capitalism's empire today signals the fall of Western civilization. However, with the word DEATH close to the reproduction of the dying warrior, human mortality may first come to mind.

Something … Perhaps a Fugue or an Elegy doesn't engage melancholy and stop at death in a traditional sense, whereby an experience of paralysis ends in utter dissolution. The work instead orients viewers toward active and creative contemplation of sad remembrance, anticipated loss, and then, unexpected gain. After all, DEATH is bracketed by bones in the assemblage (see Figure 1.2). Further, those familiar with the elegy know that it often ends in solace: Alfred, Lord Tennyson's famous 1850 *In Memoriam* was read at its publication like the

"Bible as a manual of consolation" (Poetry Foundation n.d.), and today the poem stands as a model of the hopeful elegy.

Durham suggests *Something … Perhaps a Fugue or an Elegy*'s relationship to poetry with the capacity to console in some of the words included among the assemblage's elements. Words are literal and associative in the piece, and reading them is literally a moving affair, for texts appear in the assemblage to orient its audience physically and conceptually. "STAR" and "START," along with "TOP" and "STOP," ask viewers to consider how adding things to others shifts meaning, and the placement of words at the front, back, top, and bottom of *Something … Perhaps a Fugue or an Elegy* encourages us to move across and around the piece, while scanning it upward and downward. In so doing, we are presented with another way of considering mortality than the seeming oblivion in Saramago's statement that the world forgets us when we die.

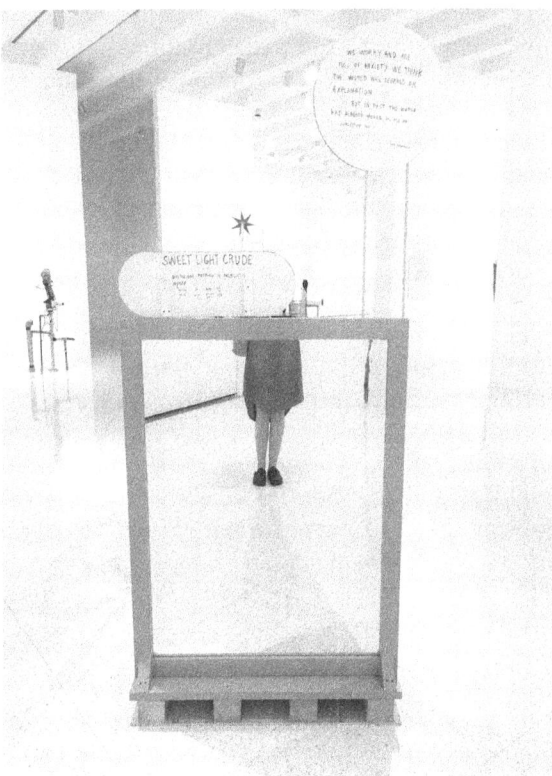

Figure 1.3 Jimmie Durham, *Something … Perhaps a Fugue or an Elegy*, detail of back section (view, Walker Art Center, Minneapolis, 2017).

Our passing is not only sad according to the assemblage, but also literally uplifting: when we look at the piece from its end, we see all but our head reflected in a mirror, with the word and form "STAR" placed where our head would be. We also read the words SWEET LIGHT CRUDE and NYMEX petroleum price quotes, a reminder that however sweet and light, we are embedded in crude extraction: oil that pollutes and death that removes. *Something ... Perhaps a Fugue or an Elegy* thereby conveys that part of us remains reflected in the world as residue both sweet and crude, and part moves beyond it – while still casting light on others. As experience and idea, the assemblage links the concrete and the immaterial conditions of life and death to individual and collective loss, and the consolation the elegy can offer.

Conceptually, physically, and emotionally moving aspects of the assemblage occur not only through language, but also alongside it with rhythm and tempo established by objects' breaks from and connections with one another; different and like colors and textures among parts and their groupings; as well as varied shapes and heights of pieces in relation to one another. *Something ... Perhaps a Fugue or an Elegy* as a composition thereby provides experiences of sensuality and knowing not only with but also without words – much like the orchestral fugue affects listeners' senses and cognition through nonverbal language. The assemblage ties European visual art, poetry, and music forms together as deeply embodied meditation on being assembled and disassembled: of civilization powerful and broken, objects used and discarded, communication direct and indirect, and lives present and past, including our own. Sorrow and consolation rippled through me and other Hammer Museum and Walker Art Center visitors with whom I spoke as we walked around thinking about and feeling our way through Durham's piece. I did not feel emotionally immobilized, nor did others with whom I discussed the assemblage, but I wondered whether our affective and cognitive experience of *Something ... Perhaps a Fugue or an Elegy* could take us anywhere else besides our own hearts and minds.

The Assemblage as a Map

The assemblage as a set of relations designates not only a medium of art, but also a conceptual term in current intellectual discourse that describes how we are thoroughly embedded in and not outside of what we experience. Part of this term's lineage arises from philosophers Gilles Deleuze and Félix Guattari's influential theory of assemblages as socio-political formations (1987).

For Deleuze and Guattari, assemblages are any sort of arrangement, including a movement, institution, or work of art. Assemblages are comprised of specific heterogeneous components and share a basic structure, but have different typologies and processes. All assemblages are an immanent array of elements shaped by a network of experienced conditions and figured by mobile positions. As typologies with particular operations, they take up varied distributions of power that reinforce or reconfigure accumulations, boundaries, and hierarchies. Deleuze and Guattari maintain that assemblages never work solely in any one way toward one end.

However, the philosophers see the greatest possibility of emancipatory relations in what they deem the nomadic assemblage. Deleuze and Guattari are inspired by nomadic peoples' lives: those shared by fellows who move from one set of conditions to others according to how they can best adapt to and shape different circumstances. The philosophers therefore define the nomadic assemblage as that which "constructs a participatory arrangement in which all elements of the assemblage enter into an open feedback loop in which the condition, elements, and agents all participate equally in the process of transformation" (Nail 2017, 33). *Something ... Perhaps a Fugue or an Elegy* as an assemblage has this character: no one part of the work dominates or transcends others; perspectives shift through movements within and around the composition; and thinking with the assemblage nudges aside a will to know it as one thing only.

Literary scholar Jonathan Flatley's notion of affective mapping provides a key to how such relational experience can be transformative – specifically, how a particular work of art activates us. Flatley develops his concept of affective mapping by re-envisioning melancholy, the affect he sees at work in novels by Henry James, W.E.B. Du Bois, and Andrei Platonov, and which envelops *Something ... Perhaps a Fugue or an Elegy* too. Flatley argues that the writers he studies mobilize melancholy to wed agential powers to critical thought and existential rumination.

Flately's argument is informed by cultural critic Walter Benjamin's historical materialism whereby melancholic reflection on the past reconfigures understanding of the present with an eye toward

creating a better future. Benjamin wrote in Europe between World
Wars I and II and sought the truth of his violent age in the literal
and figurative trash of its cultural production: broken consumer
goods that index past lives' dreams and the aestheticized politics
of fascism that ignited murderous destruction. Benjamin's writing excavates remnants of the subjugated dead's losses, wresting
them from the linear narratives written by the powerful to justify
their control. In Benjamin's work, those cast aside from before now
speak in assemblages striving for a just tomorrow. For Benjamin,
when solitary, melancholic fixation on the past shifts into active
rethinking of a present imbricated with others, connections are established, and perhaps linked to collective work for positive change
(1969, 254).

For Flatley, such a trajectory occurs with an affective map, a
sort of guide through time and space that coordinates what affects people, and how it affects them toward particular ends. If
we are to know ourselves in the past, present, and future that
Benjamin describes, an affective map has to jolt us out of sad
rumination into a more positive state. Flatley argues that this
happens through estrangement: an experience of seeing ourselves
in something, then off to its side so that we see it differently, and
understand our place in it anew. The key to such understanding
as a rudder for action lies in reorienting affect: "anxieties must be
overcome, [and] alliances must seem not just logical but emotionally compelling" (2008, 79).

Consolation as connection in *Something ... Perhaps a Fugue or
an Elegy* offers such a shift in affect: loss, decay, and death are ev-
erywhere in the assemblage – ruined lives, ruined traditions, ruined
goods, ruined socio-political relations – but the notion that none
signals finality and isolation stands firm. In *Something ... Perhaps a
Fugue or an Elegy*, the cast-off and the dead assemble as creation in
which we viewers see ourselves as literal reflections in mirrors and
figurative reflections in language. We are *in* the worst and best of
European civilization past and present, empire and art; it dies and
so do we. Saramago's text quoted in Durham's work maintains that
the world moves on without us, a quote that brings loss to its most
individual and intimate form, but the word STAR in place of our
head in the mirror image of our body at *Something ... Perhaps a
Fugue or an Elegy*'s far end suggests otherwise (see Figure 1.3). Perhaps as science tells us, and as the poet Ernesto Cadena reminds us
in his 1993 *Cosmic Canticle*, we are made from stars, and both alive
and dead, we are part of the universe that is a part of us (American

Museum of Natural History n.d.). As creation that moves us and through which we move, *Something ... Perhaps a Fugue or an Elegy* affirms that we are in and of all matter. This matters because, as the assemblage shows, what we do with what we inherit – whether the tradition of European art or an imperative to consume and discard – leaves marks. Since *Something ... Perhaps a Fugue or an Elegy* makes clear that such residue can be constructive like an elegy or destructive like garbage, the consolation the assemblage offers opens out toward responsibility.

Agency

Human destruction runs rampant today. Colonizers continue remorseless campaigns to take everything from indigenous peoples that sustain their lives and wellbeing. Institutions structured by white supremacism crush black lives. Right-wing politicians and their supporters deny migrants freedom of movement even when the latter flee horrific circumstances. Hate groups trample on the bodies and rights of ostracized groups. Cruel men abuse women, non-binary people, and children. The economically privileged protect their advantages from those who do not possess the means to achieve their desires, or even meet their needs. Climate change deniers block activists' attempts to effect responsible environmental stewardship. Energy, transportation, and pharmaceutical companies and agribusinesses pursue policies and practices that harm workers, consumers, and myriad ecosystems. Artists take up these fraught realities in many different ways that include, among others, exposing, testifying to, and intervening in conditions that crush flourishing. For example, the Occupy Museums collective creates public work that reveals art institutions' troubled relations with capital; An-My Lê makes photographs that bear witness to war's impacts and question their representations; and Tania Bruguera's "artivism" with fellow Cubans fights repressive measures in their homeland. Artists such as these show us, and/or put themselves and us directly into situations that braid together destruction, construction, and agency in unsettling ways that can feel anxious, empowering – or both.

Since the beginning of his career, Durham has done such complex work by exploring how humans damage all being and leave wreckage in their wake – broken lives, broken places, and broken entities – and by suggesting that if we re-enliven the things and relations we destroy, loss might move toward gain. Two of Durham's earliest art projects that express this ethos, his 1983 *Manhattan Day of the Dead* and 1984 exhibition *A Matter of Life and Death and Singing*, like *Something ... Perhaps a Fugue or an Elegy* combine art forms and address death. Created when Durham lived in New York and worked alongside artists from marginalized communities, these projects literally embody poetry and music as art, and invite viewers to take up death and see what it contributes to the now toward the future. *Manhattan Day of the Dead* is an installation of skull assemblages with a short text that urges readers "to remember the dead animals of this suffering island" and describes the project as ceremonies of passage for American Indians killed by government forces at the 1973 Wounded Knee demonstration, for Manhattanites killed by violent acts, and for us. Durham's 1984 skull assemblages *Wahya* [Wolf], *New York Gitli* [Dog], and *Tlunh Datsi* [Panther] in *A Matter of Life and Death and Singing* are also artworks-as-poetry-as-music. Their nature as embodied, transformative energy resonates with Durham's description of their making as a sort of dance with dead animals brought to viewers to signify poetically that what has concretely passed can be "reclaimed; death is not lost" (Stevens 2017, 291).

As a less overt manifestation of this position, *Something ... Perhaps a Fugue or an Elegy* greets viewers of contemporary art today on a world stage infinitely more unstable than the one Foster described when Durham's assemblage was made and first exhibited at the 2005 Venice Biennale. As a large array of detritus that prominently features broken, outdated technology and animal remains, *Something ... Perhaps a Fugue or an Elegy* not only underscores the abject waste of unbridled consumption but also resonates with mounting anxieties about how humans consume technology and it consumes us, and about how we farm animals, often in cruel ways, that destroy ecologies countless species depend upon. In the Anthropocene, it may not be possible to see any form of reclamation. Moreover to imagine that art has much to offer in such dire circumstances.

Lauterbach argues that although art "serves no practical purpose," it can help us constitute worth beyond what market forces promote, to "(re)align it with the rewards of independent determinations of value" (Introduction). She maintains, along with Said and Nochlin, that music, poetry, and visual art of the European tradition can be grounded in conditions that are limiting and even terrible, as well as built into creations that elicit critical thinking and doing – while sometimes providing comfort that all is not lost. With *Something ... Perhaps a Fugue or an Elegy*, all of these conditions unfurl.

References

American Museum of Natural History. n.d. "We Are Stardust." Accessed March 24, 2020. https://www.amnh.org/exhibitions/permanent/the-universe/stars/a-spectacular-stellar-finale/we-are-stardust.

Benjamin, Walter. 1969. *Illuminations: Essays and Reflections.* Edited and with an Introduction by Hannah Arendt. Translated by Harry Zohn. New York: Schocken Books.

Deleuze, Gilles, and Félix Guattari. 1987. *A Thousand Plateaus: Capitalism and Schizophrenia.* Translated and with a Foreward by Brian Massumi. Minneapolis: University of Minnesota Press.

Dezeuze, Anna. 2008. "Assemblage, Bricolage, and the Practice of Everyday Life." *Art Journal* 67, no. 1: 31–37. https://doi.org/10.1080/00043249.2008.10791292.

Durham, Jimmie. 1992. "On the Edge of Town." In *A Certain Lack of Coherence*, edited by Jean Fisher, 247–51. London: Kala Press, 1993.

Flatley, Jonathan. 2008. *Affective Mapping: Melancholia and the Politics of Modernism.* Cambridge, MA: Harvard University Press.

Foster, Hal. 2005. "At the Biennale." *London Review of Books*, August 4, 2005. https://www.lrb.co.uk/v27/n15/hal-foster/in-venice.

Fry, Katherine. 2008. "Elaboration, Counterpoint, Transgression: Music and the Role of the Aesthetic in the Criticism of Edward W. Said." *Paragraph* 31, no. 3 (November): 265–80. https://doi.org/10.3366/e0264833408000278.

Hirsch, Edward. 2014. "Elegy." In *A Poet's Glossary.* Boston, MA: Houghton Mifflin Harcourt. https://doi.org/10.1108/rr-12-2014-0353.

Kelly, Julia. 2008. "The Anthropology of Assemblage." *Art Journal* 67, no. 1: 24–30. https://doi.org/10.1080/00043249.2008.10791291.

Lauterbach, Ann. 2008. *The Night Sky: Writing on the Poetics of Experience.* London: Penguin Books. Kindle.

Martínez, Rosa. 2005. Curatorial Statement for *Always a Little Further*, 51st International Art Exhibition, Venice Biennale, June 12–November 1, 2005. http://www.universes-in-universe.de/car/venezia/bien51/eng/arsenale/text-1.htm.

Nail, Thomas. 2017. "What Is an Assemblage?" *SubStance* 46, no. 1 (Issue 142): 21–37. https://doi.org/10.3368/ss.46.1.21.

Nochlin, Linda. 1995. *The Body in Pieces: The Fragment as a Metaphor of Modernity.* New York: Thames and Hudson.

Pachmanová, Martina. 2006. "Linda Nochlin: Writing History 'Otherly.'" Chapter in *Mobile Fidelities: Conversations on Feminism, History and Visuality.* London: KT Press. E-book. https://www.ktpress.co.uk/pdf/mpachmanova.pdf.

Percy, William A. 2011. "Origins of a Famous Phrase." *Dyneslines*, May 2, 2011. https://dyneslines.blogspot.com/search?q=Marx.

Poetry Foundation. n.d. "Alfred, Lord Tennyson, 1809–1892." Accessed March 24, 2020. https://www.poetryfoundation.org/poets/alfred-tennyson.

Rothenberg, Jerome. 1993. "Ethnopoetics." In *The New Princeton Ency-clopedia of Poetry and Poetics*, edited by Alex Preminger, T. V. F. Brogan, Frank J. Warnke, O. B. Hardison Jr. and Earl Miner. Princeton, NJ: Princeton University Press.

Said, Edward. 1978. *Orientalism*. New York: Pantheon Books.

Saramago, José. 1991. *The Year of the Death of Ricardo Reis*. Translated by Giovanni Pontiero. New York: Houghton Mifflin Harcourt. Kindle Edition.

Seitz, William C. 1961. *Art of Assemblage*. New York: Museum of Modern Art.

Stevens, MacKenzie. 2017. "Selected Chronology." In *Jimmie Durham: At the Center of the World*, edited by Anne Ellegood, 288–303. Los Angeles, CA: Hammer Museum; Munich and New York: Prestel.

Wood, Michael. 2004. "The Music of His Music: Edward Said, 1936–2003." *October* 109 (July): 143–49. https://doi.org/10.1162/0162287041886548.

2 Neighbors and Faith in Community
Durham's Neapolitan *Presepi*, 2016 and Ongoing

Presepi (the singular is *presepe* or *presepio*) are Neapolitan nativities around which many Italian families and friends gather during the Christmas season, and that tourists travel to Naples to admire and purchase. They feature a grotto setting, the Holy Family, angels, magi, shepherds, and animals, as well as figures from Naples' history, fables, and popular culture – ranging from traditional food vendors to soccer stars. *Presepi* are a mainstay of Neapolitan life: they appear on permanent and temporary displays in museums, churches, shops, and civic centers. They play a big role in domestic life and city commerce: throughout the year, people buy additional components for their family *presepi* from Neapolitan artisans. Every day, especially around Christmas, countless people wander in and out of *presepi* shops that line Via San Gregorio Armeno, often called "Christmas Alley."

In 2016, Durham made two *presepi* (one is ongoing) and gave them to the people of the city where he resides part of the year. The first *presepe* awaits Naples' citizens and museum goers from all over at the Museo Madre, which showcases contemporary art, and the second attends Durham's neighbors each Christmas season outside the artist's home.

Durham and fellow artist and partner Maria Thereza Alves live in an area that abuts Naples' ancient, art-filled city center where *presepi* are made, as well as Naples' garbage-strewn central train station district, a place that many people consider dirty and dangerous. Crammed with Neapolitan shopkeepers, artisans, gang members, wealthy and middle-class international tourists, and immigrant and migrant workers of all sorts, the artists' neighborhood, like most in Naples, is a place of extreme contrasts. Its cacophony somewhat stills in the courtyard Durham and Alves share with their neighbors, people who work in small onsite or nearby enterprises. At Christmastime, when the artists host a party around Durham's

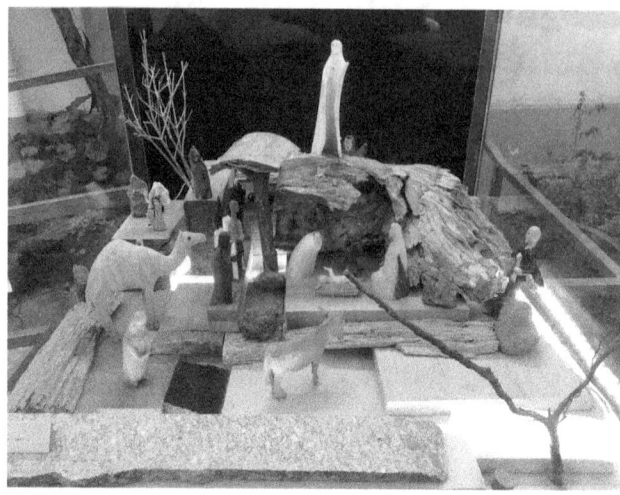

Figure 2.1 Jimmie Durham, Naples neighborhood *presepe*, ongoing, bone, cloth, Murano glass, paint, stone, wood, variable dimensions, collection of the artist (view, 2018).

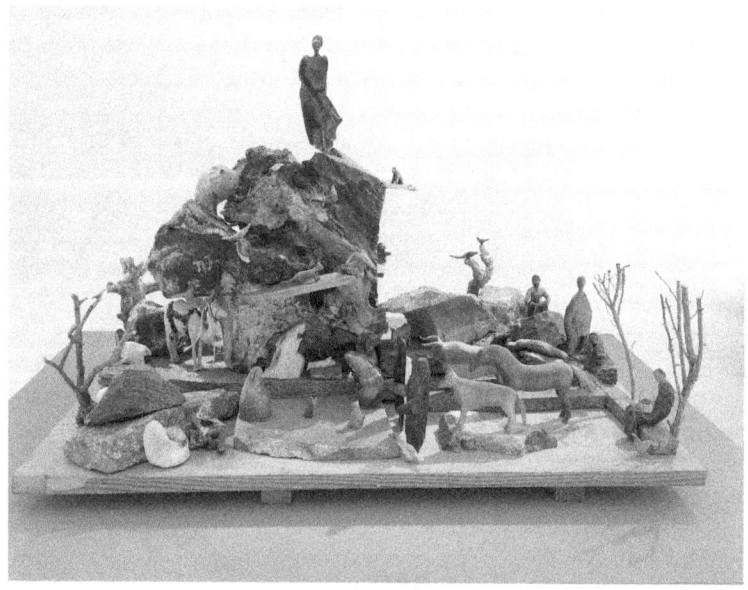

Figure 2.2 Jimmie Durham, *Presepio*, 2016. On loan to Madre • museo d'arte contemporanea Donnaregina, Naples.

presepe for these people and other friends, neighbors look to see which one of them Durham has added to the nativity in the form of a small sculpture.

Exchange among neighbors can be warm and convivial, like that among Alves, Durham, and those who surround them, but also cold and distant, or desperately fraught. In peace, neighbors can provoke jealously because of what they have, or disdain because of what they lack. In war, neighbors can betray and even murder one another to aggrandize or protect themselves. This is true of Naples: many different peoples from the ancient to the modern world fought to control it, and battles for the city rage today among organized crime gangs (Langewiesche 2012). Naples is a place of terrible economic disparity and seething resistance to migrants, and both circumstances sow hostility that fuels turmoil among those who live with one another in the city (Serenelli 2014). However, it is also a place where residents who live very different lives come together, such as in current efforts to help one another combat the coronavirus (Speak 2020).

Faith secular and sacred are forces that many in Naples draw upon to anchor the complexities and challenges they experience, and faith links some in the city while separating others. During a 2019 conference on theology and the Mediterranean in Naples, Pope Francis spoke of historical and ongoing welcome and disavowal in religious and earthly congress. Observing that the Mediterranean, and by extension Naples, have always been places "of transit, of exchanges and at times of conflict," he notes that they constitute an arena that today "raises a series of questions that are often dramatic." He queried his Naples audience:

> How can we together protect the human family? How can we foster a peaceful and tolerant coexistence that becomes an authentic fraternity? How can we get our communities to welcome the other and the one who is different from us because she or he belongs to a different religious and cultural tradition? How can religions be paths of fraternity instead of walls of separation?
>
> (O'Connell 2019)

Most of Durham's work that takes up Christianity suggests that it has produced the very problems the pope addresses. In his 2000 essay "Belief in Europe," the artist links the concepts of God and belief with a capital "B" to racism, colonization, state building, and capitalism. In the text, Durham argues that European political and economic power over people and land hinges on European belief that empires and nations bring civilization sanctioned by God to heathens and the poor – those who supposedly experience themselves within the world through "false" ritual and superstition. Durham maintains that Church and State are Belief as Law that "correctly" legislates the use of ideas, land, and all of its inhabitants – to build capital for those who best know how to serve themselves as individuals within groups governed by Law. Durham points toward what he considers better relations: participation in a hallowed world experienced through story and ritual. Not truth with a capital "T," but instead knowledge that imposed certainty cannot capture. Referring in "Belief in Europe" to animal spirits he engages, Durham maintains, "They are a group of stories, and to 'Believe' a story would be to miss it. One might learn from a story. One must Believe the Gospel. Religion means 'an organized system of dicta that are the Truth'" (2014, 174–75). Durham admired the Native American Church, which involved communal story and song during peyote use, before the church adopted mainstream Christian belief. During a 1996 interview, he set out what he values about the former, and what troubles him about the latter.

> As long as we support each other, as long as we sing our old songs and remember our history we can be free. That was the gist of every sermon with lots of embellishments and personal testimonies and that sort of churchy thing. The point was never faith in the something and then you will be free, it was we together will do our way together and then politically we will be free. In the sixties politics took over and the church went away, then in the seventies, eighties, politics were defeated and the church came back as a regular Christian church. It came back in a bad way.
>
> (Papastergiadis and Turney 1996, 49)

Durham's reflections on problems and potential promise within Christianity play out in some of his artwork. His 1989 *The Testament According to John* indicts the Christian church, while his 1992 *Jesus (Es geht um die Wurst)* explores conceptions of Christ in a more solicitous manner. The former features a phallus-cannon uttering the first words of *Genesis*: "In the beginning was the word. And the word was with God. And the word was God." Durham's image and text suggest that biblical creation begets Christian destruction bound to masculinist aggression of might as right. The artist's sculpture of Jesus also features a penis and devastation. In this instance, not to suggest unequivocal violence, but instead as a means to investigate several aspects of the human conjoined with the divine. Durham's *Jesus (Es geht um die Wurst)* explores conditions often sanitized in Christian life, specifically sex and death. The piece depicts Christ with a muddied body, blind eye, erect penis, and missing foot, holding a photograph of a box containing a decaying animal. Jesus' penis is bright red: a raw representation of male sexual readiness typical of pornography, which also evokes sexual violence committed by priests. Jesus' and the photographed animal's bodies are putrefying: their rancid decay whispers of "vermin" destroyed in the name of God, and also emphasizes the "base" materiality all share and typically fear. Durham's "ugly" sculpture defies the imperative to sanitize Christianity in image, word, and deed, beautification that strips the religion of the sensuality and physicality that make it uncomfortably and sometimes horribly human.

Jesus *(Es geht um die Wurst)* also reveals positive dimensions of "ugly" truth. Christ's face is bifurcated in Durham's sculpture. One side is a rough mixture of wood, dirt, blood, and glue, and the other side is a delicately carved and painted lovely, brown face. This visage not only reminds viewers that Jesus had dark skin and not the white flesh he typically has in Western images, but also suggests that Christ went from "dust to dust" as we do. His ruined face along with his broken body – a bone-like stick appears where one of Jesus' feet should be – demonstrate the decrepitude of all bodies, even of creatures other than us, for the photograph Jesus presents to viewers reveals the desiccated, dead animal shrouded and entombed as Christ was and human dead often are. The mud that surrounds the little creature and that enrobes Jesus too begs the question of whether we rise up from the earth, but it does not suggest that the earth devours us. The sculpture demonstrates instead that it constitutes life and death, and that it is possible to create something powerful from dirt often brushed away. *Jesus (Es geht um die Wurst)* shows viewers an embodied, brown Christ and suggests that all animals are worthy of reverence, not just humans. Jesus' red, erect penis communicates this idea with urgency: the German parenthetical title for the assemblage, *Es geht um die Wurst*, is a colloquial expression about sausage that means one must rise to a challenge right now and do one's best because the stakes are high (Müser 2015). In 1992, the stakes were very high for those crushed by the Church as Law. When Durham created *Jesus (Es geht um die Wurst)*, he and many other artists attacked celebrations of the Columbus Quincentenary as the "discovery" and making of the Americas as the New World. As a standard-bearer for the king and queen of Catholic Spain, Columbus led four expeditions to the Caribbean, Central America, and South America that paved the way for Spanish and subsequent European colonization. An ugly, decaying Christ, with half of a beautiful brown face, is a complex meditation on cruelties people have suffered in the contexts of Christianity: Christ's death because he threatened Roman power, and countless Native peoples' deaths because they threatened Western imperialism considered sanctioned by God.

The *Presepe* Tradition

Uplifting the downtrodden was at the heart of Christ's mission and taken up by St. Francis, who is credited with having invented the nativity in the thirteenth century (D'Aponte 1977). Most accounts of the *prespe* tradition say that the saint staged the first nativity with actual people and animals he loved. *Presepi* were subsequently created as objects, although live nativities continue to this day. Early fabricated *presepi* were made from stone, but terracotta, wood, wire, cloth, and paint became and remain favored materials. *Presepi* became increasingly elaborate in form and content, especially in the eighteenth century. During this period, Neapolitan secular elements joined biblical features of nativities, particularly lively street activities and tavern scenes packed with colorful characters and lush foodstuffs. Royals, aristocrats, and rich merchants competed to commission the most magnificent and elaborate nativities, not only to demonstrate their piety, but also their standing and wealth. These privileged individuals hired prominent artists and artisans, those who created large-scale sculptures for churches, to produce astoundingly life-like and exuberantly detailed *presepi*: artists painted doll-sized terracotta animals and humans with oil paint to render minute details, and clothed the latter in fine costumes made from rich fabrics and fittings (Art Institute of Chicago n.d).

The Art Institute of Chicago's *presepe*, which contains mostly eighteenth-century components, exemplifies the grandeur of the traditional Neapolitan nativity. The work is contained in a Baroque cabinet with a painted backdrop and features over 200 figures, including 50 animals, clustered in sacred and secular vignettes. Several angels draped in brightly colored, fluttering robes fly above the diorama with over a dozen putti beneath them, who mingle in Classical ruins that rise over the scenes that spill out below. The Holy Family, framed

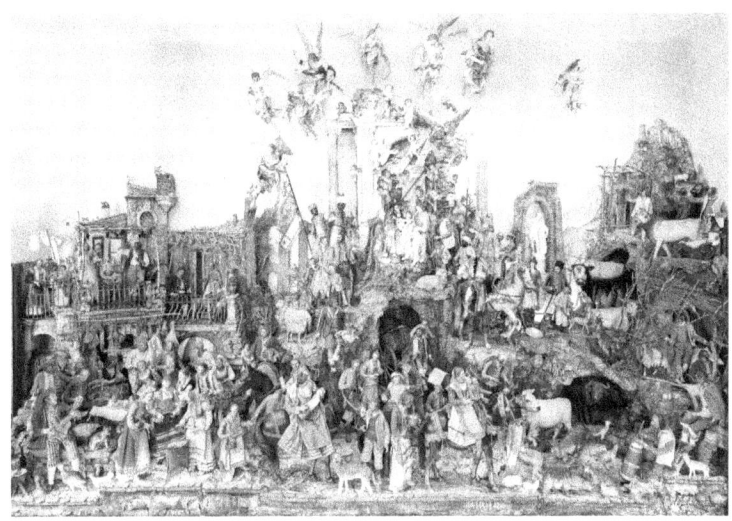

Figure 2.3 Crèche, 1725–1775. The Art Institute of Chicago.

by a Classical arch and attended by the magi, shepherds, and several domesticated creatures, rest upon a rocky outcropping around which ornately attired figures and their animal companions interact. Figures toward the left engage in work and leisure within a tavern that opens onto a street where people feast, market, and listen to a musician; and on the right, people walking and riding on horseback encounter cattle, goats, and their keepers nestled within a grotto setting. Splashes of brilliant red, vibrant teal, and soft blue punctuate an expanse of earthy brown shot through with mossy green and creamy white. Fine textures enliven the scene too, for elaborate garments flow, emoting faces ripple, and jutting rocks bulge. Packed, exuberant, and life-like, the Chicago *prespe* is a small world of realistic being, frozen in a moment of dynamic interaction.

This Baroque theatricality and ornateness remain the defining aesthetic of Neapolitan nativities up to the present (Bellenger and Romano 2016, 36–39), and realistic, elaborate, and dramatic *presepi* and their components, of varying size and quality, are available today at all price points. Shops in Naples' ancient city center sell nativity settings and elements large and small, both traditional components as well as popular culture figures. Shoppers can purchase complete *presepi* in various formats, from the Holy Family alone inside a tiny Christmas tree ornament to a village of figures with moving props ready to adorn a large table. *Presepi* storeowners also sell every imaginable individual element, at all scales, including cat-sized lambs who appear ready to gambol; fist-sized angels who seem poised to swoop; and quarter-sized movie stars who look about to sing. Neapolitan nativities have a richness that may seem at odds with the humble life their progenitor St. Francis modeled, but they have become a popular art form rather than a solely rarified art that only a few can afford. Meticulously rendered and superbly clothed magi cost a lot, but do not break the bank. Less finely crafted and more simply attired magi cost little, but still richly enhance Christmas décor. Visitors to Naples who see *presepe* for the first time invariably marvel at how different worlds collide and come together in the nativities. I saw this in 2018 around Christmas, as I experienced *presepi* in Naples churches, shops, museums, and civic centers. I saw hundreds of European, Asian, and American tourists discuss *presepi* eagerly and gaze at them in wonder.

Wonder and Good News

"It's the most wonderful time of the year" is the popular refrain from, and the title of, a song often heard at Christmastime in America. Released in 1963 by crooner Andy Williams and featured in ad campaigns for companies like Staples (Ramirez 1995), it also finds its way into carolers' repertoires. The lyrics describe happy gatherings of family and friends brought together through gifts, food, song, and "tales of the glories of Christmases long, long ago," thereby threading Christ's birth through all of its holiday celebrations to the present. Tied to sentimental images of family often linked to consumerism, the lyrics also reference the Christian miracle of Christ's birth, the inspiration for reverence, as well as gaiety and spending. Wonderful as wonder-full resonates at Christmas for those who see the nativity as both prosaic and other worldly, not as rapture in a gift card, but instead as God in an infant. For Christians, such an experience of the miraculous is religious. However, the word miraculous refers not only to the divine, but also to the extra-ordinary in the secular, that which exceeds the everyday. A tiny *presepe* baby Jesus can be a wonder: Christ materialized and/or awe inspiring artisanship. In each way, something beyond our typical experience, and likely something to spark thought – to make one wonder – as well as produce affect.

Historian Caroline Walker Bynum's understanding of wonder in the Middle Ages, which she uses as a rudder to steer her writing, sheds light on this sense of wonder as extra-ordinary experience that engages intellect. Bynum distinguishes medieval wonder (as *admiratio*), from that which emerged in the early modern world, the latter of which fueled projects to acquire places, beings, and things found beyond known horizons. For Bynum, *admiratio*, by contrast, is "cognitive, perspectival, non-appropriative, and deeply respectful of the specificity of the world" (1997, 24). She argues:

> Not merely a physiological response, wonder [in the Middle Ages] was a recognition of the singularity and significance of the thing encountered. Only that which is really different from the knower can trigger wonder; yet wonder will always be in a context and from a particular point of view. To medieval thinkers, human beings cannot wonder at what is not there; but neither can we wonder at that which we fully understand.
>
> (3)

Durham's Museo Madre and neighborhood *presepi* have these both tangible and intangible aspects of wonder, although in a manner different from traditional *presepi*. In the latter, artisans produce such realistic effects that humans, animals, and angels seem ready to spring to life. The fact heavenly host seem prepared to do so makes the supernatural, intangible for many, marvelously present. Tangibility and intangibility do not play out through illusionism in Durham's nativities. Durham does not work the materials in his *presepi* to the point of transmuting or hiding their intrinsic qualities: as with all of his assemblages, his nativities feature elements sometimes in their raw state and sometimes in part transformed. Bare or barely worked upon, the components of the Museo Madre and neighborhood nativities are resolutely there – viewers see a piece of wood, see that another is part of a wise man – but the components are often difficult to make sense of, both as material choices and as representations. Durham's *presepi* exist in the context of contemporary art, known for unusual approaches to and perspectives on creation, and they live too in the world of Neapolitan nativities where strange collisions between biblical and everyday figures can occur. However, placing Durham's *presepi* in these two contexts does not make them more graspable. It instead can compound wonder as an experience where the known and unknown intertwine: contemporary art is rarely hospitable to Christian practice and yet here it is; Neapolitan nativities rarely contain raw materials and yet here they are. Durham's *presepi* have intangible dimensions that arise within the interplay of presence and absence.

The angel figures in Durham's *presepi* are compelling combinations of the tangible and intangible: good examples of wonder in the sense that Bynum admires (see Figures 2.1 and 2.2). Viewers see the "thereness" of Durham's angels – one is clearly a white bone, and the other a mysterious, colored material that glows – but they are not present as heavenly host we know from familiar imagery. They in no way conform to the idealized naturalism and conventional beauty of angels that float gracefully above other elements in Neapolitan *presepi*. Their surprising and stunning materials as well as their strange and commanding form solicit looking in wonder and wondering: in his angels, we see "singularity and significance" that cannot be securely placed. Unlike other *presepi* that typically have several angels, Durham's nativities have only one each, and the beings do not fly. Their individuality and grounded-ness contract and intensify energy and focus, and this condensation resists charm: the artist's figures are not sweet or soothing, but penetrating and disorienting.

Durham achieves these effects with his angels using almost diametrically opposed colors, textures, shapes, and implied movement for each. His neighborhood angel is a long, white animal bone with a gap running its length in the front (see Figure 2.1). This opening not only creates a sense of lightness underscored by the angel's bright color, but also evokes a sense of absence at the figure's very material core. This incongruity is disquieting: an empty bone evokes death forcefully, and a ghost-like angel reminds us that not many people have a tangible experience of these entities. However, the sense of being and not being present, and of life and death conjoined that the angel evokes, rests at the heart of the human condition as a source not only of terrible grief, but also of inspired hope. Durham's bone angel, who seems to smile quietly, sway softly, and raise a hand gently, asks us to wonder whether what appears to be gone is entirely so.

The angel in Durham's museum *presepe* seems altogether different: it does not smile, and is not white, straight, or hollow (see Figure 2.2). Layered and sanded Plexiglas, it is solid with rounded forms, and appears to be a murky brown until hit by light: it then glows with every color of the rainbow like rich, thick glass. The museum angel is seemingly more of this world than the neighborhood angel: its form is robust, and its colors seem to capture all the elements that comprise earth, wind, fire, and water. However, like the neighborhood angel, the museum angel also evokes death: with indistinguishable features other than hollow eyes, its head looks in part like a skull, and when the figure is unlit and thus brown like dirt, it recalls the earth where bones rest. Like the neighborhood angel then, the museum angel holds life and death in tension, albeit differently. Both beings can elicit wonder as Bynum describes it: attention to difference in its specificity that compels engagement but not appropriation – the will to acquire something other, which Bynum sees in early modern endeavors. Durham's angels both exude earthly materiality and point to that which is beyond viewers' grasp.

This quality of presence and absence conveyed both in content (the angel) and in form (multivalent rather than representational), recalls philosopher, anthropologist, and sociologist Bruno Latour's meditations on what he calls "gaps of religious speech." For him, this communication exists where smooth, clear language fails to capture what goes beyond words. Latour maintains that knots and breaks characterize religious speech – a visual parallel is the odd material and awkward form that embody Durham's angels – and he argues that what may be experienced as a sort of stumbling toward the divine is the hard to convey message that what is absent is present now (2013, 105–12). For Christian believers, this can be understood as Christ's Good News: that what is far is near and that the dead live again. It is faith: the sense that the sacred is present although not concretely so in rational terms. Latour secularizes this condition of connection amidst difference and uncertainty, and does so in terms that speak to how wonder in Durham's *presepi* may enable community. Latour suggests that the "thing that turns us into individuals who are close and present might well, in certain places and in certain times, have been called 'God,' but we could also, today, just as easily call it by another vocable, such as 'The thing that begets neighbors:'" (135) that which brings what is away, near. Here, Latour is speaking of neighbors in a positive sense, as those who form a community rather than a divide.

The "thing" that brings such neighbors together has been and is variously conceived, and whether thought of as faith, love, need, or charity, support is arguably in some way at its base, as recognition, help, solidarity, or presence. Filmmaker Cristian Manzutto captured these qualities of connection in Durham's practice while filming the artist at work in his Naples studio. In the film segment, Durham arranges small sculptures he made from many cast-off materials, grouping them into arrangements of support. As he creates a little community with his creations, he points to the ways they prop one another up, showing in one instance how a sculpture leans against another to keep them both upright (Manzutto ongoing). This space of making and play is a light-hearted representation of found connection.

Toward a Provisional Whole

For Durham and Alves, animals as well as humans are neighbors: they feed feral cats that roam in their Naples courtyard, and once painstakingly nursed some of their ill kittens (Jimmie Durham, email message to the author, October 16, 2017). Animals are integral to Durham's *presepi*, possessing character that shows they are in no way subordinate to humans. Animals appear in Neapolitan *presepi*, and although some hold importance equal to many people in nativities, others are shown literally bound to humans. While buffalo and cattle are seen as entities in and of themselves, admired for their singular intelligence and beauty, respectively (Bellenger and Romano 2016, 91), monkeys and some purebred dogs in *presepi* are shown in collars, attached to aristocratic owners as emblems of wealth and exoticism (95, 159). For his Museo Madre nativity, Durham created a monkey freed from a collar and chain, and it sits high upon the ledge of a mountaintop, which is crowned by the angel and scattered with other creatures: a large bear, a cub, a ram, and multiple birds. Above the humans below, these animals emerge from the swirling, knotted wood that Durham used to create his mountain, and are themselves largely wood in various shades of lush brown. Linked together by material and color, the animals and their surroundings nevertheless have their own integrity and separateness, to which the freed monkey testifies.

Implied motion interlaces these animals with other *presepe* pieces. Each creature up high turns inward toward the Holy Family, and the camel, bull, horse, and cats on the ground at the front do the same: like the humans in the nativity, the animals focus on Christ and his parents with keen attention. Placed across and through the setting, between and next to human figures and landscape elements, the animals form with all of the other components of the *presepe* a sort of web of care. This is equally true of Durham's neighborhood nativity. In December 2018, I watched him consider where to place two people and two animals he made to add to his work, and he maneuvered them to produce a flow throughout the *presepe*, a warm dynamic that brought separate elements into a balanced composition.

A visual sense of such cohesion amidst difference in Durham's *presepi* is evident in combinations of elements that represent known and reassuring figures with others that are not: barely representational characters some may find puzzling and even distasteful. A grouping in Durham's Museo Madre *presepe* is a case in point, and perhaps for some viewers, a challenge to find connection with what may repel.

Beginning in the back, right corner of the nativity, and arcing around to the front before the Holy Family, several human, animal, and unidentifiable yet creaturely figures stand, sit, and lie in the setting. Their differences are both visual and material; yet, each is life-like, either in the sense of naturalistic representation or through material elements that in and of themselves convey energy and purpose. The contrast is especially clear in the human figures that begin and end the arc of characters: the fisherman at the back looks human, while one of the magi at the front is a misshapen blob. However, both are infused with life: the fisherman surrounded by shimmering fish bends slightly to push his net out or bring it in, and the king, an abstract entity, glows with a rich orange color that radiates warmth and vitality. Although representing a wise man as a "mere" colorful thing may appear unseemly, it suggests that illumination is infinitely more important than worldly station. Lavishing what looks to be more care on the fisherman and his fish by rendering both recognizable may seem disconcerting – they are not critical figures in nativities – but doing so makes them emblematic of the significant in the humble: the fisherman and fish are a sign of Naples itself and recall Christ as the fisher of men.

This potentially discomforting combination of approaches toward representation is more pronounced in the sweep of elements from the fisherman to the wise man (Figure 2.4).

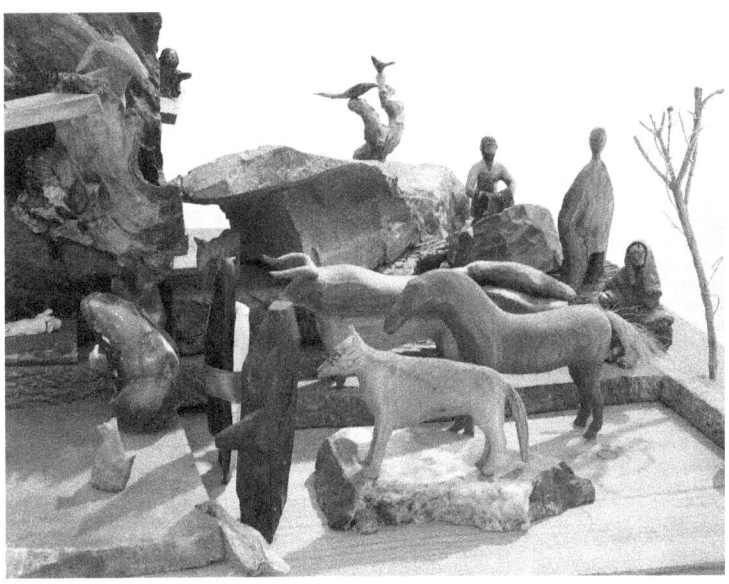

Figure 2.4 Jimmie Durham, *Presepio*, 2016 (detail). On loan to Madre • museo d'arte contemporanea Donnaregina, Naples.

A boulder to the side of a cave opening appears in front of the fisherman, and nestled between both, a long, abstracted figure lies on top of and fused with what seems to be a stone that echoes its shape. Another tall, abstracted personage, with a swelling body and featureless head, stands close to the conjoined figure and rock. A clearly defined woman with a wizened face holds a round form in one hand, and sits before both abridged characters. A male or female person in a long, dark robe – the gender is not clear as facial and hair features are minimal – sits further down from the old woman, hunched over a basket resting on its lap. Before both of these people, with items that suggest they are types of food vendors that appear in many Neapolitan *presepi*, stand a long-horned bull, horse, and wolf. Each large creature is carved smoothly from wood of different colors, with the wolf possessing the only face with features, which are taught and focused. A goose in front of the wolf is equally alert, stretched forward at the diagonal. The bird is next to two wise men behind the orange king, and like their fellow royal, they are abstract: one is an upright, dark, angular block form, and the other is a smooth, almost black, truncated staff-like element with what appears to be a curved bone bound to its back by bright blue ribbon. Two small cats sit to the left of the kings, and like all of the characters within view of the manger, they attend to the Christ child and his parents. Amidst this arc and sweep of entities that move in toward the Holy Family, beings of all sorts reside, and they exist in varying degrees of realism and abstraction, made from materials ranging from assorted woods to glass and bone. This variegated bow of the clear and the strange is disconcerting. Why is there a wolf with the bull and horse? Why is there a prone, abstract figure attached to a rock with another barely human thing nearby?

Perhaps because the wild exists alongside the domesticated, and because people are elemental, then less so as we pass from life. Durham does not tame his materials and figures, but instead focuses on their qualities and the information they can suggest rather than deliver indisputably. He produces a tension between the given and the made, showing the beauty of materials in and of themselves – the grain of wood, the glow of glass – and his careful, discreet work with them. Durham does not put virtuosity on display: we do not see figures so life-like and gorgeous that we marvel at his skill. Instead, he emphasizes his work *with* creation: give and take between what he finds and what he wants to make and see. And what we see is conjoined difference even more pronounced than that evident in Neapolitan *presepe* with traditional nativity figures and others such as movie stars, politicians, and revered athletes. In Durham's *presepe*, there is a place alongside the divine not only for representations of the secular, such as people in his neighborhood, but also for negative associations attached to cast-off materials and the near illegibility of abstraction.

While in Naples at Christmastime in 2018, I had the opportunity to experience both of Durham's *presepi* and how people interacted with them. I visited the Museo Madre and studied Durham's nativity there, examining its figures and their arrangements with other museum visitors. I overheard a young American couple describe the *presepe* as "blasphemous" because it contains "junk" and ugly portrayals of the Holy Family. They turned away from the nativity abruptly. I watched an elderly visitor from Rome approach the piece having observed the Americans' reaction, and saw him examine the piece closely. A group of Neapolitan teenagers on a school trip stopped to discuss the *presepe* with him when he asked them what they thought of it. Together, they opined about the figures' identities, materials, and arrangements, and reached no shared conclusions about them, except one which made all of them smile: that they like hearing the different ideas each had about the nativity.

That afternoon, when I left the museum, I went to Durham's studio to watch him finish new figures for his neighborhood *presepe*, pieces that represent a young girl from the area as well as a local artisan at work at his bench. Durham carefully painted the two wooden figures, and then painstakingly assembled the little workbench from a tiny piece of wood and four matchsticks. Later that evening, when Alves and Durham welcomed their neighbors and other friends to their courtyard party to see the nativity and enjoy cake and Prosecco, I watched people of all ages and backgrounds study and talk about Durham's *presepe*. Some from the neighborhood laughed when they recognized people they knew in the work, praised Durham's carving skills, and puzzled over his choice of certain materials for particular figures. A local art student told me about his family's *presepe* and wondered if they would accept contributions from him, especially if they were as nontraditional as Durham's pieces. Other students joined our discussion, which centered on speculations about what different figures represented and how things extra-ordinary can lead to thinking and evaluating.

At the Museo Madre and Durham and Alves' courtyard, this played out variously. The American couple said "no" to Durham's museum *presepe* and the art student before Durham's neighborhood nativity presumed his parents would reject something like it too. The teenagers and elderly man, and those with whom I spoke at the party, said "yes" to the artist's *presepi* even while disagreeing about what they contain. The nativities' strangeness – "crude" elements such as detritus and indecipherability – turned some viewers away and brought others forward, and not only into dialogue with the *presepi*, but also with other people.

For the Jewish philosopher, theologian, and educator Franz Rosenzweig, a capacity to welcome increasingly more of what is other into "we" facilitates neighbor-love. Rosenzweig's neighbor-love is not abstract, universal love, or surrender of self to the other, but instead concrete, shared "speech-thinking," a "tool of unification that does not reduce different individuals to that which is the same: speech only unites those who recognize or understand each other" (Pollock 2019). Rosenzweig argues that speech-thinking arises from revelation, an event that shifts a person into openness to a new positive relation, a particular impactful encounter that may lead to others.

Modern Germanic Studies scholar Eric L. Santner draws on some of Sigmund Freud's theories about internal and external lives to flesh out Rosenzweig's understanding of how positive relation can occur and expand amid otherness. Through Rosenzweig, Santner views God, world, and person as interactive being constituted and shaped through dynamic exchange. Drawing on psychoanalytic concepts, Santner maintains that the self continually navigates institutionalized and internalized defense mechanisms against the "too much" of the world in relations. These mechanisms include norms that hem in, fantasies that afford escape, exclusion that expels, and violence that destroys. Santner suggests that God is the call to be alive in and not cordoned off from the world, to be open to and work with all of it, and thereby to alterity in others and ourselves. For Santner, this connection is what makes neighbors – not tolerance of difference, or production of sameness – but instead being with and addressing our own discordance and others as moving toward a "universal-in-becoming" (Santner 2001, 7–9). This is not an idealized, already conceived universal. It is neighbor-love as an ongoing, situated process and grounded practice through which beings together compose a provisional community where dissonance reverberates but does no harm.

Compositions are configurations of varied elements into groupings that their creators find appropriate. This is the work of art, and according to philosopher Isabelle Stengers, for philosopher, mathematician, and Christian Alfred North Whitehead, it is creation more broadly: activity *with* God whereby we adjust what is given, which is often dissonant, into a meaningful arrangement. In her careful reading of Whitehead, which she describes as "thinking with" him, Stengers shows that Whitehead brought God and/ as creation – all being, all making – into relationship through "all-inclusive, unfettered valuation" (2011, 483). When everything is considered, however troubling it may be, everything coexists, and people make sense of this mass by arranging it in a manner that they take to be right.

For Whitehead, "the aesthetic value of discords in art" (475) is a microcosm of this macrocosm. Artists draw together material, process, content, context, and audience to produce work that resonates with themselves in some way, and those who come to the work do the same. "Discords in art" can exist among relations within and outside the work, as discords can in other communities, and how they are valued or not speaks to where neighbors exist for some.

Durham's *presepi* resonate in the philosophical, theological, and aesthetic registers Rosenzweig, Santner, Whitehead, and Stengers explore to think about uniting disparate being. Much like Naples itself and its *presepi*, Durham's *presepi* feature combinations of things people may find discordant, and either ugly or beautiful as such. For some of the latter viewers, his nativities occasion an encounter with provisional wholeness in conjoined difference—however one may conceive. of and experience it. While representing faith in community – Catholic devotion in a city that embodies creation and destruction in all its forms – Durham's *presepi* embody faith *in* community through art. This is a project to make neighbors of unlike and often dissonant things within art itself, and around art for viewers who value what is composed. Such a project can always fail, but sometimes succeeds. When it does, perhaps it is an example of what Politics Studies scholar Anne McNevin sees in art: "a basis from which to claim that other worlds are not a utopian horizon, but part of lived reality – albeit in partial, fragmentary and incipient forms" (McNevin 2020).

References

Art Institute of Chicago. n.d. "Neapolitan Crèche: A Holiday Gift to the City." https://www.artic.edu/exhibitions/3219/neapolitan-creche-a-holiday-gift-to-the-city.

Bellenger, Sylvain, and Carmine Romano. 2016. *The Neapolitan Crèche at the Art Institute of Chicago.* New Haven, CT: Yale University Press.

Bynum, Caroline Walker. 1997. "Wonder." *The American Historical Review* 102, no. 1 (February): 1–26. https://doi.org/10.2307/2171264.

D'Aponte, Mimi Gisolfi. 1977. "*Presepi*: A Neapolitan Christmas Ritual." *Performing Arts Journal* 2, no. 2: 49–60. https://doi.org/10.2307/3245336.

Durham, Jimmie. 2014. "Belief in Europe." In *Waiting to Be Interrupted*, edited by Jean Fisher, 174–75. Milan: Mousse Publishing; Antwerp: M HKA.

Langewiesche, William. 2012. "The Neapolitan Mob's Most Dangerous Family." *Vanity Fair*, April 10, 2012. https://www.vanityfair.com/culture/2012/05/naples-mob-paolo-di-lauro-italy.

Latour, Bruno. 2013. *Rejoicing: Or the Torments of Religious Speech.* Translated by Julie Rose. Cambridge, UK and Malden, MA: Polity Press.

Manzutto, Cristian. ongoing. *Jimmie Durham* (documentary in process).

McNevin, Anne. 2020. "Borders, Migration, and the Urgency of Imagination." *Vacarme*, 89/cahier, February 16, 2020. https://vacarme.org/article3308.html.

Müser, Kate. 2015. "Germany's Best Sausage Expressions." *DW*, September 29, 2015. https://www.dw.com/en/germanys-best-sausage-expressions/a-18717394.

O'Connell, Gerard. 2019. "Pope Francis to Theologians in Naples: One Cannot Do Theology without Freedom." *America: The Jesuit Review*, June 21, 2019. https://www.americamagazine.org/faith/2019/06/21/pope-francis-theologians-naples-one-cannot-do-theology-without-freedom.

Papastergiadis, Nikos, and Laura Turney. 1996. *On Becoming Authentic: Interview with Jimmie Durham.* Cambridge, UK: Prickly Pear Press.

Pollock, Benjamin. 2019. "Franz Rosenzweig." *The Stanford Encyclopedia of Philosophy*, edited by Edward N. Zalta. https://plato.stanford.edu/archives/spr2019/entries/rosenzweig/.

Ramirez, Anthony. 1995. "A Wacky Campaign Pushes the Envelope for Abrasive Humor." *The New York Times*, January 26, 1995. https://www.nytimes.com/1995/01/26/business/media-business-advertising-wacky-campaign-pushes-envelope-for-abrasive-humor.html.

Santner, Eric L. 2001. *On the Psychotheology of Everyday Life : Reflections on Freud and Rosenzweig.* Chicago, IL: University of Chicago Press. https://doi.org/10.7208/chicago/9780226734897.001.0001.

Serenelli, Luigi. 2014. "In Italy, Immigrant Surge Raises Tensions in South." *The Washington Times*, December 24, 2014. https://www.washingtontimes.com/news/2014/dec/24/in-italy-immigrant-surge-raises-tensions-in-south/.

Speak, Clare. 2020. "Fundraisers and Balcony Singalongs: How Italians Are Rallying Together Amid the Coronavirus Crisis." *The Local*, Italian edition, March 13, 2020. https://www.thelocal.it/20200313/fundraisers-volunteering-and-balcony-singing-how-italians-are-rallying-together-amid-the-coronavirus-crisis.

Stengers, Isabelle. 2011. *Thinking with Whitehead: A Free and Wild Creation of Concepts*. Translated by Michael Chase. Cambridge, MA: Harvard University Press.

3   Civilization and Its Dis(Contents)

Maria Thereza Alves and Jimmie Durham's *The Middle Earth*, 2018

In the Introduction to her translation of Homer's *The Odyssey*, classicist Emily Wilson reflects on civilization and how it is inflected through relations and words in Homer's Mediterranean epic. She considers what and who is monstrous in this regard by considering functions of exclusion in *The Odyssey*.

> Before approaching the island of the Cyclopes, Odysseus tells his men that he has to find out some important information: whether the inhabitants are "lawless aggressors," or people who welcome strangers. Odysseus presents these categories as if they are mutually exclusive: the willingness to welcome strangers is figured as enough, in itself, to guarantee that a person or culture can be counted as law-abiding and "civilized." The Cyclopes would have good reason to be suspicious of these visitors, who have looted and slaughtered the inhabitants of the previous island that they visited. But the dichotomy hints at the importance in *The Odyssey* of *xenia*, a word that means both "hospitality" and "friendship." The cognate word *xenos* can mean both "stranger" and "friend"; it is the root from which we get the English word "xenophobia," the fear of strangers or foreigners, as well as the sadly less common "xenophilia," the love of strangers or of unknown objects.
>
> (2018, 23–24)

Wilson's observations speak to the situated nature of relations. Strangers known to be aggressors merit distrust, and how to address those known to be in need, as well as those unknown, are questions. The foreign and dangerous along with the like and beloved course throughout *The Odyssey* in which "The tension between strangeness and familiarity is in fact the poem's central subject" (ibid., 4). This tension plays out in how *xenos* manifests as polarized binaries or conjoined differences – through which power as domination or life force courses.

In 2018, Nathalie Ergino, director of the Institut d'art Contemporain, Villeurbanne near Lyon, invited Alves and Durham to use the institute and ancient objects from regional museums to create a project about the Mediterranean past and present. The resulting exhibition, *The Middle Earth*, consisted of adjacent rooms filled with inter-connected creations, some of which incorporated sound, taste, smell, and touch, as well as sight. Alves and Durham's show featured objects and texts, as well as food, plants, and music. Little known information about and unexpected things from the Mediterranean informed the artists' arrangements of their exhibition components, which together shed light on how the region has been and is experienced and understood by different people.

The Middle Earth filled the institute's nine rooms (the first has an extension), and North and South Halls, all of which flow in a circular pattern. Each space was painted a specific color; housed ancient artifacts; pieces made by the artists or collections of objects in their possession; fragments of largely vintage illustrated books; and texts on the walls that named each space and provided scientific names of animals and plants. With respect to the latter, the larger words designated animals and the smaller identified plants, with the placement of each word often suggesting the height at which one might encounter the particular beings in their environments. The lack of corresponding images of these beings suggests how scientific discourse can be a distancing operation that sometimes fails to see vital conditions.

Alves and Durham named each room according to the theme or subject they addressed in the identified space. Room One explored food and music, and the room's extension addressed borders. Room Two investigated writing, Room Three examined dye, and Room Four concerned glass. The North Hall contained Alves' installation on the Siren (Figure 3.1).

Room Five looked at the temple and its relationships to the Mediterranean, and Room Six accommodated Durham's installation *Mediterranean Sea*. Room Seven examined flint, the South Hall addressed plants, Room Eight investigated trees, and Room Nine considered iron. Thus, Alves and Durham explored the Mediterranean's historical and current conditions in terms of specific materials, technologies, and lifeways, drawing on systems of knowledge and practice that speak to experience in the region today.

The booklet written by museum staff that accompanied the exhibition describes the artists' project as a poem about the human condition: an aesthetic, metaphorical representation of stages and processes that unfolded and continue to unfold in the site often taken

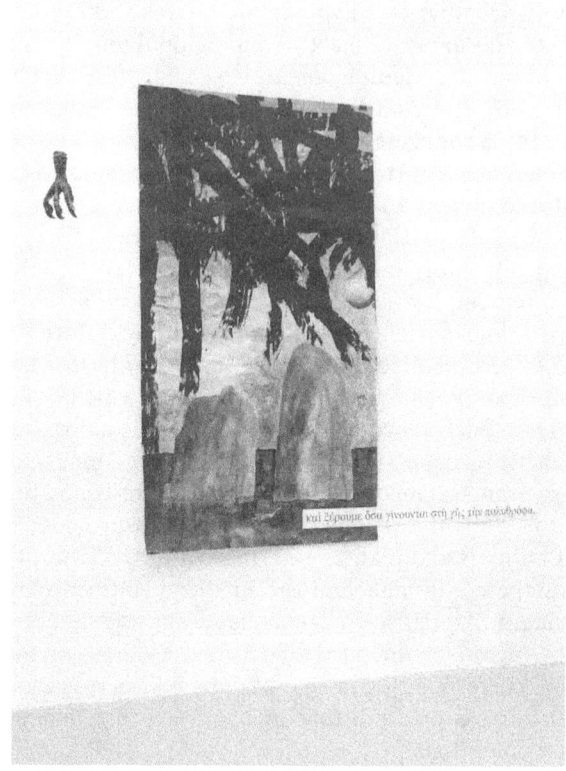

Figure 3.1 Maria Thereza Alves, *We Know Everything That Happens Over All The Generous Earth*, 2018, glass, watercolor, paper, sound, inoxydable glass, acrylic paint, participation: Yoali yescas amaro, variable dimensions, collection of the artist. View of the exhibition The Middle Earth – Mediterranean Project of Maria Thereza Alves & Jimmie Durham, Institut d'art Contemporain, Villeurbanne, France (March 2–May 27, 2018).

to be the cradle of Western civilization. The booklet also notes that Alves and Durham took four beings as their guides when creating their three-dimensional poem, entities disappearing from memory or the earth itself (Institut d'art Contemporain, Villeurbanne 2018). Visitors encountered three of these guides in the first room of the exhibition: the Corbezzolo, or strawberry tree in English, the Mediterranean monk seal, and the hermit ibis. The fourth guide, the murex, appeared in Room Three dedicated to dye (Figure 3.2).

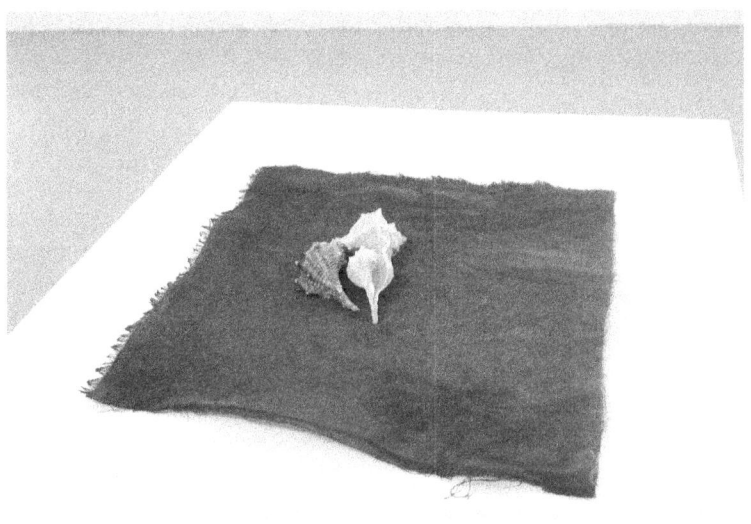

Figure 3.2 Jimmie Durham's murex collection, 24.5 × 22.2 × 2.5 cm. View of the exhibition *The Middle Earth* – Mediterranean Project of Maria Thereza Alves & Jimmie Durham, Institut d'art Contemporain, Villeurbanne, France (March 2–May 27, 2018).

Although not stated in the material designed to help visitors orient themselves within the show, the part human, part animal Siren of the North Hall was also a critical figure in *The Middle Earth* (see Figure 3.1). She served as a potent embodiment of women's power in life and death, and a pointed reminder that beings – human, animal, and otherwise – downplayed or excluded in accounts of the Mediterranean in fact often instantiate its conditions.

Each room of *The Middle Earth* examined mythological, historical, and contemporary conditions of the Mediterranean through various entities and processes both destructive and creative. Alves and Durham combined different material and temporal registers in their exhibition to make the European narrative of heroic Greco-Roman "whiteness" fade into the luminous color of varied being that makes the Mediterranean. Like the Mediterranean of the past, the region today encompasses diverse and complex ecosystems, ethnicities, and worldviews. In *The Middle Earth*, Alves and Durham created a microcosm of the Mediterranean where differences, often demon-ized in today's virulently nationalistic world, come together and also tear apart.

Alves and Popular Aesthetics as Politics

The aesthetic-conceptual force of Alves' practice animates *The Middle Earth*. A multimedia artist who works with a wide range of materials ranging from clay and glass to photographs and video, Alves collaborates with many partners, including students, indig-enous communities, seeds, and plants. Her art and that which she has made with others take shape not only in forms well established in the art world, but also in formats such as the garden and dictio-nary. Alves' 1999-on *Seeds of Change* explores the politics of colo-nial exchange through gardens: she plants them in port cities with seeds discovered in dumped merchant ship ballast, and does so to make visible and grow little known consequences of uproot and transfer. Her 2010 *Dicionário Krenak–Português/Português–Krenak* helped revive the Krenak language: she facilitated translation of an almost lost indigenous tongue out of Portuguese and into the lives of people determined to fight Brazilian policies that devas-tate their communities. Alves displays her work in combinations of texts, images, objects, and often growing things. Her installations are not slick, nor formalist, regularly employ materials many would consider humble, and typically feature information that describes opposition to degradation. She sometimes uses satire to skewer op-pression, but when foregrounding resistance, she treats her subjects with earnest respect. Alves' projects always expose, illuminate, and tackle injustices about which she provides facts and propels action.

From Brazil and of indigenous, African and European descent, Alves has lived as well as made art about colonization's ongoing dire impact. In her 2017 "A Question of Aesthetics and Colonization," Alves clearly states how her politics inform her aesthetic approach to art. Her text appears in an issue of the journal *OnCurating* that asks artists, curators, and researchers how art institutions can be decolonized. Alves describes in her essay how as a young political organizer and artist in Brazil she was shut out from art institutions: she couldn't show her work because she wasn't from an upper-class family and refused powerful men's sexual advances; and she didn't enter a museum to study art because its elitist design, purportedly democratic, was intimidating. She contrasts these experiences with those she has had since 2009 with the Museo Communitario del

Valle de Xico, a community museum established for and by immigrants from all over Mexico who settled on land outside of Mexico City (13–15). Spanish industrial magnet and land developer Íñigo Noriega Laso created this land in the late nineteenth century for European-style agriculture and did so by desiccating Lake Chalco. This ecocide crushed the lifeways and livelihoods of over 24 indigenous villages and towns, and Noriega's private army removed thousands of people from the region and forced others into labor (Castro 2006, 60; Alves 2012; Emmelhainz 2017, 52–53). Today, the region is sinking and flooding, while its clean aquifer is pumped away. Alves worked with the Museo Communitario to document this history and its effects in clear, accessible arrangements of photos, texts, and models, and to recreate a *chinampa*, an indigenous artificial island engineered for hydro-agriculture that fed countless indigenous people before Spanish colonization.

In "A Question of Aesthetics and Colonization," Alves notes that in 2014, when she exhibited an installation about her collaboration with Museo Communitario in Mexico City's Museo Universitatro Arte Contemporaneo, some Museo Universitatro staff felt that her work wasn't art because of its "popular aesthetics." Her answer to *OnCurating*'s question about how to decolonize museums is also a critique of traditional beauty in art: she affirms her commitment to multidisciplinary, collaborative, political art designed with the beauty of a democratic, conceptual aesthetic. She wrote: "How to decolonize the museum? Staff that have a colonial idea of art can retire to Europe and the Museo Comunitario del Valle de Xico, can take over" (14). Alves not only argues for her method and how it is physically and visually embodied, but also maintains that decolonization is institutional change and not only new knowledge production. Many indigenous peoples and their allies call for this work, arguing that European colonization of the Americas through genocide, land theft, resource extraction, and forced assimilation began a process that continues through settler colonial nation-states that naturalize claims to place (Mignolo and Nanibush 2018, 24–29). Political Science and Indigenous Studies scholar Glen Coulthard, a member of the Yellowknives Dene First Nation, suggests that decolonial work within specific places can literally ground better relations for those crushed by European praxis in colonized sites.

> I would like to think of ground, literally, as the grounds of solidarity between struggles. We should be thinking about how it's been used to divide and conquer us, to segregate us, to

displace us from our communities, our homes, and in Indigenous peoples' case their traditional territories. So our analysis of solidarity and resistance ought to be one that highlights how multiple forces interact with one another and how to overcome them through these strategic acts of solidarity. I think this is not just a theoretical question to be debated in the academy; it is being played out beautifully on the ground....

(Gardner and Clancy 2017)

Alves' pursuit of decolonization through her art does this work, and it intersects with Durham's commitment to indigenous rights and critical analysis of Euro-American systems of domination. Since meeting in 1978 when Alves volunteered to work at the AIM International Treaty Council office Durham ran in New York, the artists have not only worked individually, but also together, and at times with others, to make art that challenges colonialism's cruelties. One of their best-known joint projects is *Virginia Veracruz/Veracruz Virginia* with Alan Michaelson, a Mohawk member of the Six Nations of the Grand River. The three performed this piece in 1992, during the 500th year anniversary of Columbus' voyages, which launched Europe's incursion into the Americas. Alves, Durham, and Michaelson together roamed Madrid while wearing muzzles, suggesting that silenced American Indians are (at) the very ground of colonization – the site of campaigns to erase Native peoples while taking their land and its resources to build up European power centers such as Madrid.

When Alves and Durham moved to Europe two years after this project, they added another political dimension to their work: they looked at Europe's internal histories and their intersections with global politics. In 2008, Alves and Durham created with anthropologist Michael Taussig *The Museum of European Normality*, modeled after documentation centers designed to inform visitors about particular regions and their populations. The museum included Alves' satirical 2008 *Tchám Krai Kytõm Pandã Grét/Male Display Among European Populations* and 2007 *Fair Trade Head*, biting ethnographic studies of European practices – of men touching their genitals in the first case, and museums collecting indigenous peoples' remains in the second. The installation also featured poignant materials, including several maps that show migration patterns across Europe, and an "anti-guest book" with over 5,000 names of people who died trying to immigrate to Europe or in refugee camps designed to contain them (Manifesta 7 2008).

This compassionate dimension of Alves' popular aesthetic committed to justice undergirds the *The Middle Earth*. The approach relays information clearly, affirming an accessible attitude to display like that developed by her community partners rather than seemingly disinterested exhibit modalities that emphasize elegance over substance. Alves is sensitive to her subjects, materials, and audiences, and affords dignity in representation to everyone and everything often considered disposable. *The Middle Earth*'s look and feel breathed Alves' popular aesthetic born of justice in action.

Alves' artistic process, which often begins with an investigation of specific wrongs, dovetails in *The Middle Earth* with Durham's, which typically begins with an investigation of specific materials and how they solicit critical thinking about troubling realities. These starting points move Alves and Durham into conceptual ground born of shared politics. Both creators reveal and criticize humans' destructive interactions with one another and all being, and thwart in their art – through materials, subjects, and practices – the categories and hierarchies that steer this harm. Alves and Durham disavow punitive boundaries and discriminatory chains of being, and embrace sentience and non-sentience in all of its manifestations as well as creation in all of its forms. For the artists, animals, plants, and natural elements are as valuable as all humans, and artisanal expertise, fine art practice, manual labor, and research share pride of place and often work synergistically. This ethos is at the heart of *The Middle Earth*. Alves and Durham invited an array of being into the exhibition and mobilized the breadth and depth of their practices to produce a multidimensional, affective, critical reflection on the Mediterranean, one shaped by Alves' popular aesthetics.

Orientation and/as Invitation

All of *The Middle Earth*'s components together destabilized the visual and physical arrangements typically employed in the West to put an environment "in its place": the map, illustrated reference, chart, classification system, museum display, canonical mythic account, and news report. Room One established this approach: food offered on tables, chairs provided for sitting, music playing for welcoming ambiance, and colorful objects distributed through space to delight the eye all invited viewers to become participants in putting together sensory and cognitive understanding with the artists, versus passively acquiring knowledge through seemingly objective, didactic display. As I moved through the galleries shortly after they opened to the public, I saw this former logic unfold, and attended carefully to how viewers interacted with the exhibition spaces, the artists' work, and one another. People took food, listened to music, read texts, studied objects, touched plants, and spoke with one another, sharing opinions about ideas their experiences activated.

Alves and Durham first nudged me and other visitors to *The Middle Earth* into a critical, active role by ushering us into an encounter with problematic modes of understanding alongside a model for shaping knowledge differently. The latter is *Mediterranean*, a brilliantly colored mosaic made by the artists from detritus, some of which they collected from the shores of the Mediterranean Sea (Figure 3.3).

Among the first works visitors saw upon entering the exhibition, *Mediterranean* hung where the initial space one encountered moved into the second. A visual invitation into *The Middle Earth*, the piece also serves as a conceptual key to the show: a guide to how sensuous and cognitive experience can combine to offer insight and

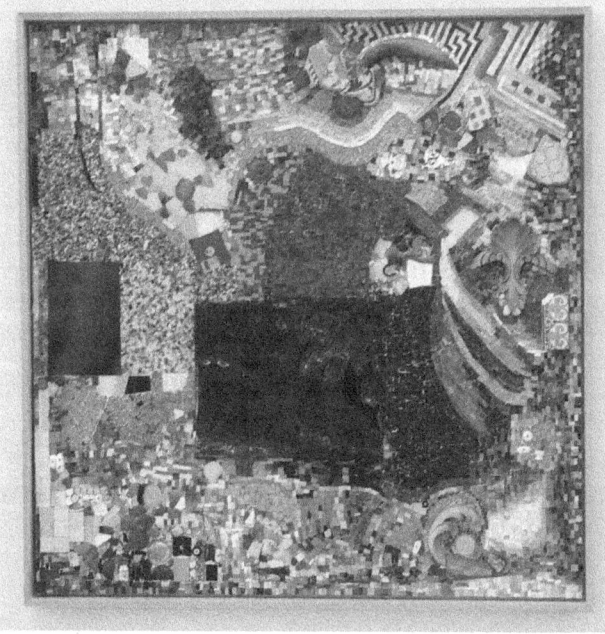

Figure 3.3 Maria Thereza Alves and Jimmie Durham, *Mediterranean*, 2018, mosaic, mixed media, 156 × 156 × 9 cm, collection of the artists. View of the exhibition *The Middle Earth* – Mediterranean Project of Maria Thereza Alves & Jimmie Durham, Institut d'art Contemporain, Villeurbanne, France (March 2–May 27, 2018).

inspire thought. *Mediterranean* takes up what has been cast aside and arranges it as a connected dissimilarity: detritus combines in a freeform arrangement with dynamic, abstract shapes of varying sizes and colors, most of which are as bright as the yellow walls of the room that housed the mosaic. Line, color, and form in Alves and Durham's *Mediterranean* refuse clear demarcation that signals value and use; instead, thrown-away pieces of broken glass, wood, and consumer goods produce a patterned web of relations. *Mediterranean* does not represent or resemble a particular thing, presenting instead a dynamic, connective logic very different from that evident in the other large visual array in Room One: *Mittlemeerländer*, a 1986 German physical and political map of the Mediterranean.

The map is a product of the Justus Perthes publishing house, which since 1809 has produced atlases and maps that have shaped geography as a discipline and practice in government and education (Linke, Hoffmann, and Hellen 1986, 75). The map provides highly detailed visual information about topography, hydrography, as well as political and administrative units: line, color, form, and language divide place into spheres of control and influence. Alves and Durham placed carefully chosen fragments of illustrated books alongside the map to underscore this controlling logic. Two fragments to the left in one case chart a route through Algeria and Libya, and in the other, depict what appear to be French colonial administrators seated in front of black "charges." A line drawing of a robed woman in a town of the Côte d'Azur labeled a "lesson" in identification, and the first page of a colloquium paper comprised the two elements to the right of the map. The paper is titled "The Phytogoegraphical Delimitation of the Mediterranean Region towards the East," and it contends with how to identify and label three regions with African and Middle Eastern peoples.

European maps typically establish a God-like view of regions carved into nation-states conceived in ethnic terms. *Mittlemeerländer* and the fragments Alves and Durham put on either side of it reveal this impetus, for each separates Mediterranean lands and peoples into distinct, racialized entities. This is a product of colonization and the work of Orientalism, meshed European beliefs and practices that Edward Said argues turns peoples of the "Orient" – today's Middle East, North Africa, and Asia – into Europeans' devalued "Others" (1978). Orientalism threads throughout European knowledge systems: official illustrated texts and academic papers like those that frame *Mittlemeerländer* regularly label places and their inhabitants in line with racist socio-political frameworks. In the first room of *The Middle Earth*, Alves and Durham established their commitment to thwarting this sort of freighted, hierarchical spatial organization filtered through the lens of visual control. The artists did so not only by critiquing European mapping practices, but also by inviting varied sensory encounters with food and music into visual experience. This invitation suggests that knowledge can combine different experiential elements to nourish minds and bodies, perhaps producing vital connections like those figured in Alves and Durham's mosaic.

Welcoming

Alves and Durham's welcome to visitors echoed another call to welcome, a statement they hung in the space of transition between Room One and the further rooms that contained their exhibition. Titled "The Human Condition," the statement addresses the historical and current conditions of Europe and migration. The artists' text notes that Europeans have histories of perpetrating horrific injustices by invading and colonizing other places and also of escaping injustices in their own lands by immigrating elsewhere in search of freedom. The statement observes that the Americas became home to millions of European immigrants, lands colonized by their forbearers, and that most of these immigrants embraced myths of European superiority that they passed down to their descendants. Stating that like all peoples Europeans are inherently neither good nor bad, and that a nation's decisions do not always reflect the convictions of their citizens, Alves and Durham's text proclaims that migrants to Europe today must not be viewed as illegal aliens but instead as the free people European immigrants thought themselves to be. The artists' words point to the cruelty and hubris of Europe's refusal to welcome at its Mediterranean borders African, Middle Eastern, South Asian, and other migrants who flee places torn by colonization, war, and ecocide. Alves and Durham end their statement by honoring "those who, right now, courageously meet up at Europe's frontiers and who will help construct the future" (2018).

That future is hard to image, for today's Mediterranean migration is shattering. Thousands of migrants from Africa, the Middle East, and South Asia have died, and more are dying, attempting to reach Europe via the Mediterranean Sea in order to escape "chronic poverty, political instability, wars, and the climate crisis in countries often laid to ruin" by "the legacy of colonialism and the west's military machinations" (Hsiao-Hung 2020). From 2009 to 2018, approximately two million migrants entered Europe by crossing the Mediterranean through one of three routes: Turkey to Greece, Morocco to Spain, and Africa to Italy. The number of people who passed through these routes up until 2018 varied based on pressures both external and internal to Europe. About 1.2 million migrants fleeing armed conflicts in Afghanistan, Iraq, and Syria arrived in Greece, but the number decreased in 2016, when Turkey agreed to accept migrants in exchange for financial assistance from the European Union. About 780,000 migrants from North and Sub-Saharan Africa fleeing desperate military and economic situations arrived in Italy, but fewer came in 2018 when the Italian government pursued draconian immigration policies, denying port to boats with migrants, and partnering with the Libyan Coast Guard to take back migrants and prevent them from leaving Libya in the first place. About 89,000 migrants entered Spain fleeing abuse and hardship in Africa and the Middle East, but arrivals picked up in 2018 when Spain allowed ships with migrants to dock after they were denied entry elsewhere (Connor 2018). That year, the Africa to Italy route became deadlier than at any point since the peak of Mediterranean migration in 2015: during the first seven months of 2018, when *The Middle Earth* was on view, 1 in 18 migrants drowned trying to reach Italy. Activists and NGOs have helped and continue to help migrants in danger at sea and on the ground, but right-wing measures to keep migrants out of Europe prevail (Kingsley 2018). Although one of Europe's most powerful anti-immigration politicians, Italy's Matteo Salvini, was voted out of office in 2019, the EU nations have not been able to devise a coordinated policy on migration, reach agreement about how to respond to migrant humanitarian crises throughout the Mediterranean (Butini 2019) or quell xenophobia.

European narratives of one union and/or one nation for its "rightful" citizens, conceived in terms of race and ethnicity, erase historical and present evidence of fluid human relations in Europe, particularly in the Mediterranean, the site often viewed as the birthplace of Western culture and the most contested region of migration in Europe today. Canonical histories of Europe recount nations' political and cultural achievements – in light of their supposed fidelity to Greek and Roman philosophy, governance, and art – as expressions of universal history and world civilization (Weller 2017, 11–12). In such texts, Greek and Roman history is firmly rooted to Europe, and scrubbed of its debts to beliefs and practices of Mediterranean peoples of today's North Africa and

Middle East. This literally whitewashed Greco-Roman European ideology arose in part from the eighteenth-century Enlightenment belief in progress as scientific discovery and encyclopedic classification, sifted through "civilizing" colonization, which was ennobled in Neoclassical textual, visual, and spatial representation. Europeans viewed peoples of Africa, the Americas, Asia, the Middle East, and the Pacific as objects of study and use from inferior cultures (Outram 1995, 63–79). The eighteenth- and nineteenth-century Grand Tour, which rounded out the privileged European man's education as visits to civilization's most noteworthy Classical sites (Opper 2003, 60–66), followed by a professional posting as a colonial administrator, exemplifies this logic. Remnants of this praxis diffuse today through museum exhibitions that portray Western art by white males as the best of civilization and "non-Western" creations as "ethnic objects" of scientific and/or aesthetic interest.

As critical museum display, *The Middle Earth* intervenes in this history and participates in an expanding effort propelled by artists, museum professionals, and academics to rethink European art and exhibitions in light of migration and its impact on Europe. During 2011–15, researchers based at The University of Naples "L'Orientale," located in an ancient city once and now populated by the Mediterranean's diverse peoples, contributed to the MeLa project, which evaluated European museums in an age of migration and culminated in a report about museum programming that challenges narratives about Europe as the West and not the "Rest." Naples researchers Iain Chambers, Lidia Curti, Alessandra De Angelis, Beatrice Ferrara, Giulia Grechi, Celeste Ianniciello, Mariangela Orabona, and Michaela Quadraro argued in a MeLa report that "Migration, accompanied by transnational exchange, is transforming the museum from a static site of archiving and conservation into an active space for engendering encounters with further, often repressed, stories and memories" (MeLa 2015, 24). That artists drive much of this work is clear from Ianniciello's research on artists such as Lara Baladi, whose representations of movement rupture simplistic, prejudicial constructs of Middle Eastern experience; Mona Hatoum, whose installations map, reconfigure, and destabilize boundaries in the Middle East and world at large; and Emily Jacir, whose art in public spaces gives voice to Arab and Palestinian histories erased in nationalist narratives. For Ianniciello, these creators are a few of many at work in the Mediterranean who provide "perspective[s] with multiple shards of telling and understanding the world, a spectrum of voices and gazes from different bodies of experiences and lives" (2018, 80).

Alves and Durham's *The Middle Earth* does similar work: it examines and breaks down conceptual schemes that produce normative representations of the Mediterranean as white Europe. The artists' statement about Mediterranean migration challenged viewers to see Europe as Eurasia, a continent occupied by diverse peoples divided by borders that have shifted and hardened through power relations. Alves and Durham's text about migration hung across from a chart with the alphabets of Mediterranean peoples past and present. The chart's beautiful Egyptian, Canaanite, Ugaritic, Phoenician, Greek, Etruscan, Aramaic, Hebrew, Arabic, Berber, Greek, Russian, Armenian, Georgian, Latin, and English letters demonstrate how many varied people have lived and continue to live in the Mediterranean. The letters' similar and different looks, as well as their translatability, point to connection within difference among the Mediterranean's populations. Below the chart, two cases contained ancient male and female figurines without features that would identify them as a particular ethnicity. This evidence of non-prescriptive human representation contrasted markedly with modern stereotypical Middle Eastern and North African figures in fragments of illustrated guides or textbooks affixed to walls. Another fragment with a drawing of a leopard and an exchange between a "gentleman" and a "brigand," in which the latter gives the former his coat, made it clear that Alves and Durham wanted their visitors to move through *The Middle Earth* without "judging a leopard by its spots."

This link between the human and animal played out in other ways in the exhibition, and in each instance, welcomed animals into the spectrum of difference that constitutes the Mediterranean. In addition to establishing metaphorical connections between animals and humans, Alves and Durham examined mythological human-animals, and revealed their own connections with animals who served as their guides for creating *The Middle Earth.* In Room One, the hermit ibis appeared in an Alves painting that captured the bird's distinctive look: the creature has a black, spiky feathered ruff surrounding a bald head with a long, curved red beak. Alves' painting hung not far from a small, ancient Egyptian wooden boat with two passengers, reminding viewers that the ibis was sacred to Egyptians, for whom the bird symbolized fertility, virtue, and life after death (deKramer 2018). The second animal guide in Room One was the Mediterranean monk seal, represented by a replica skull of the creature accompanied by a text the artists wrote that links the seal with the Siren in Homer's account of Odysseus. The ancient Greeks saw the Siren as a half woman-half bird being, later represented as a mermaid, who lures sailors to their death with irresistible songs. Alves and Durham noted in their statement about the monk seal that it sings, and therefore may have been the Siren that many imagined haunted Mediterranean shores. Alves' installation about the Siren further in the exhibition explored this animal-female's power. Bound to life and death, as well as fact and story, the hermit ibis and Mediterranean monk seal guides point to the value of being in multiple forms – living creature, felt spirit, mythological entity, and artistic representation – each of which engages the past and present in different registers, both affective and cognitive.

Alves and Durham's focus on animals in the context of migration between myth and real-world conditions speaks to their perception of myth and reality as always intertwined. The artists showed viewers of *The Middle Earth* that what we take to be a myth about animals could be real: an experience of animals as concrete, guide-companions. With respect to migration in today's world, the artists drew exhibition visitors' attention to myths that demonize migrants and veil the historical conditions that made immigrants of persecutors' ancestors. Alves and Durham's statement about migrants at the Mediterranean borders of Europe today makes evident their commitment to permeable physical as well as conceptual boundaries through which crossings enable thriving and not devastation.

The artists underscore this possibility in the garden Alves designed for *The Middle Earth*. As with many of her art garden projects, Alves arranged potted flowering herbs, shrubs, and small trees into a composition of which one becomes a part. Some plants rested on a bench in the shape of an S-curve where exhibition goers were able to sit, listen to Alves' *Chanson Florale* (a recorded song with seven parts), reverberate through the space, and watch the play of light and shadow through the floor length windows that brought the outside into contact with the inside. Fragments of illustrated texts on the wall informed readers that beloved fruits and vegetables with Lyon in their names, such as the Lyon peach, like other plants were brought from elsewhere to France where they became "naturalized" additions to people's diets and gardens. Alves and Durham's invitation to reflect on this knowledge while sitting amidst such plants and listening to multiple voices harmonize made clear the artists' invocation to welcome further "transplants" who can nourish Europe: the migrants often kept at or turned away from Europe's borders.

Alves and Durham painted the space that housed the garden a light yellow, a softer version of the bright yellow on the walls of the room that invited exhibition goers into *The Middle Earth*. Between each yellow area, visitors passed through rooms painted various colors, with blue standing out. Most colors were a subtle mix of one hue with white that produced soft, luminous shades with a pink, beige, gray, or green cast, and as visitors moved within and across rooms, shifts in lighting made the wall colors change. These experiential effects communicated two key ideas: that color enriches and changes whiteness, which as light is itself composed of different colors, and that multiple possibilities exist within different vantage points. Sharp shifts in color, from the barely violet-white of Room Five focused on the temple to the blue of Durham's installation *Mediterranean Sea*, reinforced the experience of *The Middle Earth* as a three-dimensional version of Alves and Durham's *Mediterranean* mosaic that visitors saw when they entered the show (see Figure 3.3). Moving through colored spaces that shifted in hue produced an aesthetic-conceptual experience of variation and change as shared mobility. Displays of objects, images, and texts, as well as spaces for rest and nourishment encouraged me and other exhibition goers to experience ourselves as active learners through thinking, contemplating, and socializing. Progressing through a visual and physical array with rich information about interaction in the Mediterranean, I became with other exhibition visitors part of a literally moving critical reflection on the complexity of exchange in the region. We were a three-dimensional version of the artists' mosaic *Mediterranean*: our multiplicity and difference together created a flow that metaphorically represented that of others who in the past were, and in the present are, the Mediterranean.

Matter and Mattering

Movement and corporeality intersected with physical qualities of matter and mattering in Room Two dedicated to writing, in which Alves and Durham broke down divisions between fine and decorative art, as well as written and spoken language in order to emphasize the communicability of all materials. The room featured examples of cuneiform cylinder seals and writing, accompanied by a statement that explained how Mesopotamian artisans wrote transactions into wet clay with cylinder impression seals made from semi-precious stone worn as necklaces. Nearby, Alves and Durham provided another statement about beads, in this instance, how they were used for communication in a spiritual rather than secular vein. The statement noted that Islamic prayer beads came to Greece when the Turks occupied it, and Catholic rosary beads arrived in Greece when it became Christian. Durham's *Pleas in Stone*, a long string of semi-precious, variously colored stone beads, featured an invitation to touch material that helped past peoples of today's Middle East and Greece communicate with one another and God. This physical encounter, which mirrored *The Middle Earth's* linked flow of colored rooms, provided exhibition visitors with a tactile experience of how matter matters.

While the ripple of color throughout the exhibition's spaces and across *Pleas in Stone's* length produced felt, physical bonds among different elements, color also signaled tension when it highlighted exhibition components that addressed histories of iniquity and reflections on violence. The communicative and physical qualities of color as connection as well as cruelty played out in Room Three dedicated to dye. In this space, Alves and Durham addressed the material and social conditions of royal purple, also called Tyrian purple, and *porpora* in Italian, the latter of which is also the name of the artists' joint painting of a large square of this color. Visitors confronted this square in conjunction with two other purple squares: one, a small photograph of Queen Elizabeth in purple dress affixed to a wall, just above the floor, and the other, a cloth on top of a pedestal, upon which three murex shells rested (see Figure 3.2). A text about Tyrian purple accompanied these triangulated elements and brought their relationships into sharp focus. Phoenicians of Tyre, from the ancient world through the Middle Ages, made rich purple dye from murexes. They did so by collecting untold numbers of the mollusks – tens of thousands were necessary to make enough dye for a small swatch – stripping the creatures from their shells, then drying the animals and boiling them. The process produced a horrific stench but resulted in a rich, vibrant color that intensified rather than faded over time. Tyrian purple was enormously expensive, even more precious than gold, and became an index of prestige and power worn only by the richest and most powerful people from the ancient to the medieval Mediterranean (Cooksey 2013). Today, murexes are almost extinct, not only because of over harvesting, but also because climate change has compromised their marine environments (Beaumont 2016).

Durham says that materials are innocent, but what we do with them is not (2014, "Artist Talk"). This is glaringly apparent with Tyrian purple. The murex was the third sprit guide for Alves and Durham in *The Middle Earth*, and the artists' three purple squares set up a tribute to the creature almost eradicated to make a color that marks hierarchy and wealth. The artists literally elevated murexes by placing their shells on a pedestal, putting an image of a queen in purple below them, and freeing the color itself into a painting of purple alone. This display in Room Three, in conjunction with those in Room Two, showed viewers that humans work with the stuff of the world in both beautiful ways, as with writing and beads, and in ugly manners, when we cruelly use beings like the murex for aggrandizing purposes.

Durham's installation *Mediterranean Sea* in Room Six emphasized how humans destroy what we are given, and do so with what we make. The *Mediterranean Sea* was an immersive experience: exhibition goers stepped down, into, and up from the installation, a space with soft blue paint on the walls and garbage strewn across the floor. The walls also contained the names of sea creatures along with words about plants and the early origins of the sea. A small statement informed viewers that the earth once consisted of a north and a south continent, five large families of plants that birthed many more that we know today, and a sea called Tethys by geologists. The Greek goddess Tethys was the mother of the waters and nymphs, and the beauty of growing life on earth that Durham evoked by referring to her and all that she sustained withered amidst the ugly, raw garbage that claimed the space visually and physically. Because the *Mediterranean Sea* occupied a room below Rooms Five and Seven, spaces viewers saw behind and before them while traveling the one path through the installation, Durham produced the effect of submersion – the sense of being within the Mediterranean Sea as the Middle Earth itself. This actual sea passage today is not only littered with garbage, but also with the bodies of migrants who tried but failed to flee destructive circumstances. Metaphorically submerged within a sea that gave life and that now dies swallowing human castoffs, both literal trash and people treated as such, exhibition visitors were faced with a quiet but powerful reckoning. We were able to move up and out of the *Mediterranean Sea* and this physical ability to remove ourselves from implied suffocation communicates the privilege of safety and freedom we know that those kept from Europe do not.

Listen to the Siren

Alves' installation in the institute's North Hall, *We Know Every-thing That Happens Over All The Generous Earth*, also addressed the Mediterranean Sea as a site of destruction alongside creation and did so through the figure of the Siren (see Figure 3.1). The work consists of a suspended, just over life-sized, black-green glass bird foot with talons, and a large-scale painting that shows Odysseus' boat off in the distance between huge rocks, with long, black, clawed brushstrokes raining down from above and a full breast emerging from the right side. The piece also features a haunting soundtrack with a plaintive female voice that sings, keens, and yelps all at once. The cry reverberated through the hall that contained Alves' installation, and as viewers moved into and through the space, the painting with sculpture had rippling effects as well. From several vantage points, the glass, clawed foot stood out starkly against light beige walls, gleaming subtly; from other perspectives, the three-dimensional talons merged with those in the painting, adding force to the aggressive sweep of black that threatened the tiny boat below. The single breast, clearly visible amidst the flurry of black strokes, along with the single clawed foot, emphasized the woman-bird nature of Sirens, and suggested their destruction too.

Highly sexualized today as femme fatales, transformed into se-ductive mermaids in popular representation, the Sirens of ancient Greece manifest differently and variously. In vase painting and sculpture, they occur as birds with women's heads or upper bodies, with birds' legs, and with or without wings. In myth, their story associates them with music, allure, knowledge, and promise. They are often described as Persephone's playmates, given wings by her mother Demeter to fly quickly to rescue her daughter from Hades. This legend maintains that the Sirens were unable to do so, and settled on a rocky Mediterranean shore, singing to those who sailed by to join them and hear their song of knowing all that happens. In Homer's *Odyssey*, Circe warned Odysseus that the Sirens lured sail-ors to their deaths with their enticing voices, so he had his sailors lash him to his ship's mast, so he could hear the Sirens but also stay on course. Legend maintains that the women-birds were fated to die if rejected and did so upon diving deep into the sea, becoming sunken rocks. Because they were associated with death, enchant-ment, song, and eloquence, sculptures of Sirens appear on an-cient Greek tombs and funeral monuments for orators, poets, and women and girls considered lovely (Struck 2020). In Greek myth and life, the Sirens were multidimensional, infinitely more than the seductive, evil destroyers of heroic men who populate modern and contemporary imagery. Alves' installation makes this multivalence explicit and gives power to the Siren, making Odysseus a mere footnote in her story: he does not appear in the artist's painting and is only referenced by his small ship at the bottom of the artwork. The single breast in the piece points to possible sexual allure, but its shape and color closely resemble those of the small islands Odysseus sails between, evoking the rock the Sirens will become after death instead of flesh that may excite. Alves' painting's black, claw-like strokes as well as her glass claw afford the Sirens great, raptor-like strength, while the haunting cry the artist provides, offsets the aggression with lyrical potency. The song winds its way through many of *The Middle Earth*'s rooms, thereby keeping the dismembered Sirens alive alongside their enjoinder to "know with them everything that happens over all the generous earth." These luminous words, as the title of Alves' representation of the Siren, run as separate, large Greek text across the bottom and outside of the artist's painting's frame. In Room One, next to a reproduction of the Mediterranean monk seal's skull, Alves and Durham placed a statement that links the seal's voice with that of the Sirens' beautiful lyrics. Folding the death and the song of a mythological female creature into those of an endangered seal that served as Alves and Durham's guide, the artists moved destruction and creation through life and art, the known and the unknown. The Siren's very mutability as loss and/or gain opens out onto the possibility of knowledge as replete as the very earth itself.

This generous understanding of Siren song is markedly different from how the ancient Greeks understood female sound, which they associated with loss and animalism in negative terms. Poet and classicist Anne Carson explores these connections in a poem from the seventh century BCE by Alkaois, a writer exiled from the assembly of men to the female island of Lesbos. He mourns his loss of work among male authorities, bemoaning his life amidst "wolfthickets" inundated by the "shrieking" sound of women during a yearly festival.

> The wolf is an outlaw. He lives beyond the boundary of usefully cultivated and inhabited space marked off as *polis*, in that blank no man's land called to *apeiron* ("the unbounded"). Women, in the ancient view, share this territory spiritually and metaphorically in virtue of a "natural" female affinity for all that is raw, formless and in need of the civilizing hand of man. So

for example in the document cited by Aristotle that goes by the name of The Pythagorean Table of Opposites, we find the attributes curving, dark, secret, evil, ever-moving, not self-contained and lacking its own boundaries aligned with Female and set over against straight, light, honest, good, stable, self-contained and firmly bounded on the Male side (Aristotle, *Metaphysics*).

(1995, 122–24)

Alves' installation thwarts ancient Greek prejudice that associates the woman with all that is in need of control, prejudice that remains deeply embedded in masculinist praxis to the present. The artist's hybrid woman-bird-seal is not either/or, but instead and-and-and. The Siren crosses boundaries and cannot be bound: her song of knowledge, which echoed throughout the three-dimensional exhibition mosaic of which visitors were a part, is that great harm ensues when people demonize what can be known of the generous earth – when we move away from what we take to be dangerous but may not be. Philosopher and Religious Studies scholar Pamela Sue Anderson argues alongside countless other feminists that difference registers in the West through gendered binaries such as male/female, culture/nature, human/animal, history/story, as well as fellow/other, and that these strictly bounded forms contract thought, stifle creativity, and constrict or destroy what is feminized and devalued. Anderson argues that when feminists retool myths, protean understanding itself subject to mutation, they

> … make manifest what content has been excluded from the more narrowly rational construction of … beliefs. By content is meant, besides empirical or intellectual intuition, such material dimensions of reality as … one's physicality…. myth and mimesis can serve as philosophical tools for feminists who endeavor to transform the patriarchal structures of empirical realist forms…. This includes structures which constitute sexual, racial and ethnic hierarchies of privileged vs. less-privileged beliefs…. mythical configuring and mimetic refiguring enable unsettling entrenched positions. This means positions which remain especially difficult to dislodge, since reason has been conceived as disembodied (male) and as such superior…
>
> (1996, 115)

Alves' *We Know Everything That Happens Over All The Generous Earth* encapsulates the work of *The Middle Earth* as a whole: that the Mediterranean can embody shared, creative knowledge that sustains and it can instantiate restricted, destructive ignorance that crushes. Alves and Durham provide visitors with the opportunity to see themselves directly in these possibilities. Before leaving *The Middle Earth*, visitors entered in Room Nine, a semi-enclosed, circular space that housed an Etruscan mirror. Although tarnished bronze, the mirror reflects back one's self, an experience made contemplative in the round, intimate space. The sense of seeing oneself in the past was then shifted into seeing oneself now moving forward, for opposite the Etruscan mirror stood *Self-Imposed*, a wood assemblage with a mirror at eye view, which lined up with the doorway that led back toward the exhibition's beginning and exit. Visual and symbolic self-reflection as a felt physical passage through colored space returned visitors to the bright yellow Room One filled with food and music – and the mosaic *Mediterranean* (see Figure 3.3). After watching exhibition guests of many ethnicities and backgrounds eat together while discussing how they made sense of the show, I saw that for those of us free to be in Europe amidst powerful art, it is possible to leave *The Middle Earth* nourished, thinking that the Mediterranean has been, and sometimes is, a place of many different parts that fit, as well as a site of ruin. How nation-states and concerned collectives of the Mediterranean respond to migration crises and ecological destruction now and moving forward will determine who and what come together and fall apart in Europe. Or, more properly, as *The Middle Earth* shows, Eurasia.

References

Alves, Maria Thereza. 2012. *The Return of a Lake*. http://www.maria-therezaalves.org/works/the-return-of-a-lake?c=24.
———. 2017. "A Question of Aesthetics and Colonization." *OnCurating* no. 34 (December): 13–15. https://www.on-curating.org/issue-34.html#.XoEKqIhKiUk.
Alves, Maria Thereza, and Jimmie Durham. 2018. Artist Statement for *The Middle Earth*, Institut d'art Contemporain, Villeurbanne, March 2 – May 27, 2018.
Anderson, Pamela [Sue]. 1996. "Myth, Mimesis and Multiple Identities: Feminist Tools for Transforming Theology." *Literature & Theology* 10, no. 2 (June): 112–30. https://doi.org/10.1093/litthe/10.2.112.
Beaumont, Peter. 2016. "Ancient Shellfish Used for Purple Dye Vanishes from Eastern Med." *The Guardian*, December 5, 2016. https://www.theguardian.com/environment/2016/dec/05/ancient-shellfish-red-mouthed-rock-shell-purple-dye-vanishes-eastern-med.

Butini, Cecilia. 2019. "There's Still No Plan to Deal with Migrants in the Mediterranean." *The Nation*, November 1, 2019. https://www.thenation.com/article/migrant-mediterranean-salvini-rescue/.

Carson, Anne. 1995. *Glass, Iron and God*. With an Introduction by Guy Davenport. New York: New Direction Books.

Castro, José Esteban. 2006. *Water, Power and Citizenship: Social Struggle in the Basin of Mexico*. Houndmills, Basingstoke and New York: Palgrave Macmillan Publishers Ltd.

Cooksey, Chris. 2013. "Tyrian Purple: The First Four Thousand Years." *Science Progress* 96, no. 2: 171–86. https://doi.org/10.3184/003685013x13680345111425.

Connor, Phillip. 2018. "The Most Common Mediterranean Migration Paths into Europe Have Changed Since 2009." Pew Research Center, September 18, 2018. https://www.pewresearch.org/fact-tank/2018/09/18/the-most-common-mediterranean-migration-paths-into-europe-have-changed-since-2009/.

deKramer, Karyn. 2018. "Northern Bald Ibis – (Geronticus eremita)." Artists for Conservation "Silent Skies" Project. http://gallery.artistsforconservation.org/artists/1028/conservation/project/northern-bald-ibis-geronticus-eremita.

Durham, Jimmie. 2014. "Artist Talk." Filmed June 12, 2014 Video at Parasol Unit Foundation for Contemporary Art, London, in Conjunction with the Exhibition *Jimmie Durham: Traces and Shiny Evidence*. Video, 38.04. https://parasol-unit.org/whats-on/jimmie-durham-traces-and-shiny-evidence/.

Emmelhainz, Irmgard. 2017. "Chronicle of a Visit to the Museo Comunitario del Valle de Xico, Or: Cultural Solidarity in the Globalised Neoliberal Age." *Afterall: A Journal of Art, Context and Enquiry* 43 (Spring/Summer): 46–57. https://doi.org/10.1086/692553.

Gardner, Karl, and Devin Clancy. 2017. "From Recognition to Decolonization: An Interview with Glen Coulthard." *Upping the Ante: A Journal of Theory and Action*, August 2, 2017. https://uppingtheanti.org/journal/article/19-from-recognition-to-decolonization/.

Homer. 2018. *The Odyssey*. Translated and with an Introduction by Emily Wilson. New York and London: W. W. Norton & Company. Kindle.

Hsiao-Hung, Pai. 2020. "The Refugee 'Crisis' Showed Europe's Worst Side to the World." *The Guardian*, January 1, 2020. https://www.theguardian.com/commentisfree/2020/jan/01/refugee-crisis-europe-mediterranean-racism-incarceration.

Ianniciello, Celeste. 2018. *Migrations, Arts and Postcoloniality in the Mediterranean*. New York and Abingdon: Routledge.

Institut d'art Contemporain, Villeurbanne. 2018. *The Middle Earth – Mediterranean Project of Maria Thereza Alves & Jimmie Durham*. Villeurbanne, France: Institut d'art Contemporain, Villeurbanne.

Kingsley, Patrick. 2018. "Mediterranean Death Rate Is Highest since 2015 Migration Crisis." *The New York Times*, September 3, 2018. https://www. nytimes.com/2018/09/03/world/europe/mediterranean-migrants-deaths. html.

Linke, M., M. Hoffman, and J. A. Hellen. 1986. "Two Hundred Years of the Geographical-Cartographical Institute in Gotha." *The Geographical Journal* 152, no. 1 (March), 75–80. https://doi.org/10.2307/632940.

Manifesta 7, the European Biennial of Contemporary Art. 2008. *The Museum of European Normality* by Maria Thereza Alves, Jimmie Durham, and Michael Taussig. http://www.manifesta7.it/artists/489.

MeLa Project. 2015. *RF02 – Cultural Memory, Migrating Modernity and Museum Practices.* http://www.mela-project.polimi.it/upl/cms/attach/20160204/151021620_3748.pdf.

Mignolo, Walter D., and Wanda Nanibush. 2018. "Thinking and Engaging with the Decolonial: A Conversation between Walter D. Mignolo and Wanda Nanibush." *Afterall: A Journal of Art, Context and Enquiry* 45 (Spring/Summer): 24–29. https://doi.org/10.1086/698391.

Opper, Thorsten. 2003. "An Ancient Glory and Modern Learning: The Sculpture-Decorated Library." In *Discovering the World in the Eighteenth Century: Enlightenment,* edited by Kim Sloan with Andrew Burnett, 58–67. Washington, DC: Smithsonian Books.

Outram, Dorinda. 1995. *The Enlightenment.* Cambridge, UK and New York: Cambridge University Press.

Said, Edward. 1978. *Orientalism.* New York: Pantheon Books.

Struck, Peter T. 2020. "Sirens," Mythology website. http://www.classics. upenn.edu/myth/php/tools/dictionary.php?method=did&regexp=91& setcard=0&link=0&media=1.

Weller, Charles R., ed. 2017. *21st-Century Narratives of World History: Global and Multidisciplinary Perspectives.* Cham: Palgrave Macmillan.

4   Animals Are Our Brethren

God's Children, God's Poems, 2017

In 2017, Heike Munder, director of Zurich's Migros Museum für Gegenwartskunst, invited Durham to exhibit at the museum *God's Children, God's Poems*, a group of 14 large assemblages that he made with the skulls of Europe's biggest mammals: the Alpine ibex, bison (wisent), brown bear, Great Dane, elk, Eurasian lynx, Manx Loaghtan, Maremmana bull, musk ox, reindeer, Shire horse, wild boar, and wolf. Durham enhanced the skull of each creature with various materials such as glass, leather, and paint, and produced a body for each animal from items such as machine parts, furniture elements, and building components. Durham's sculptures stood at the height of the animals they embodied, and filled an entire, expansive gallery.

Durham is known for making art with animal skulls, especially pieces he exhibited in the early 1980s in New York City. Like all of Durham's work, these 1980s animal skull assemblages address the history and present circumstances of place. US lore represents Manhattan as the site American Indians supposedly traded to colonizers for beads; it is also the site where Durham and many other activists battled for indigenous rights at the United Nations headquarters. Durham's 1982 untitled baby buffalo skull piece and 1984 assemblages *Wahya* [Wolf], *New York Gitli* [Dog], and *Tlunh Datsi* [Panther], the first part of the installation *Manhattan Day of the Dead* and the others part of his show *A Matter of Life and Death and Singing*, acknowledge American Indians' powerful presence and continuity in the face of terrible losses. The skull works are enlivened with colorful beads, shells, stones, feathers, and paint. With vibrant materials often linked to traditional Native cultures, especially the skull of the animal most associated with Indians, Durham's baby buffalo piece and three other skull sculptures index vigorous ongoing life among peoples and lifeways that many Americans take to be dead. In the nineteenth century, the American government attempted to exterminate Plains Indians by destroying the buffalo, their revered animal kin and life source, and horrifying evidence of this attempted genocide of people and animals remains in period photographs of armed American men standing on huge mountains of bison skulls. Durham's wolf, dog, panther, and especially baby buffalo skull artworks from the 1980s take on this attempted American annihilation and counter it with power accrued from death speaking back to life.

Durham's 2017 project with the skulls of Europe's largest animals faces death and life in another specific context: Europe's both impassioned and dispassionate relationships with animals, including humans. In the essay he wrote for the *God's Children, God's Poems* exhibition catalogue, Durham explains that the title of his show contains translations of the old Greek terms for animals, and "God's children, God's poems" suggests that they are beloved family alongside humans, creatures who possess the evocative strength of poetry and spiritual existence (2017, 12). Powerful entities in the myths and histories of Eurasian peoples, including the Greeks and Romans, as well as "barbarians" – indigenous European peoples who brought down the Roman Empire – animals have also functioned in Europe as food sources, domestic companions, hunting trophies, natural history specimens, and entertainment in fighting matches, fairs, and zoos. Many animals today, including some whose skulls appear in *God's Children, God's Poems*, are disappearing from earth because people destroy their environments. Agribusiness fuels much of this loss in Europe, as elsewhere, and does so when domesticated animals, largely cattle, are farmed for meat and milk on land poisoned by fertilizers and pesticides that once sustained other species. *God's Children, God's Poems* greeted viewers in Switzerland and this nation's popular image as stupendous alpine lands dotted by small farms that produce famous cheese seems to belie the dire conditions of agribusiness. However, Basel-based Syngenta is one of the world's largest producers of pesticides and genetically modified seeds linked to extreme environmental ills (Pesticides Action Network 2017). Thus, although Switzerland has perhaps the world's most progressive legislation on animal rights (World Animal Protection n.d.), its business sector contributes to the decimation of species around the globe. Popularly conceived as a country free from the harm associated with much of Europe's reach into the world, Switzerland has its dark side as well as its light. Durham's exhibition *God's Children, God's Poems* in a country famous for neutrality in war suggests that no place is actually neutral when it comes to destruction.

Thinking and making with the skulls of Europe's largest animals, in *God's Children, God's Poems*, Durham extended his commitment to explore how we shape and are shaped by the matter of our world – the entities we live among and the materials we produce – and what matters to us as things come into and pass from existence. In this framework, Durham's skull assemblages ask viewers to address two particular, inter-related questions. First, how might we honor what we have lost in one dimension and gained in another? Second, if we are able to do this, how might it enrich our relationships with others as we move further into the Anthropocene?

These are important and timely questions, and *God's Children, God's Poems* provide powerful means to engage them by encouraging those who experience Durham's animals to reimagine separation and connection. These two conditions register forcefully in *God's Children, God's Poems* for some of the creatures involved – such as the rare, four-horned Manx Loaghtan and the huge Maremmana bull descended from extinct aurochs – are unfamiliar and strange, but their postures and arrangement invite relationship with one another, as well as with people who regard them. Some of Durham's animals works loom, a few confront, and others range alongside, with each possessing eyes that draw viewers in while directing them outward too.

Durham calls his skull assemblages "animal spirits," thereby situating their presence at the place where life and death meet, the visible and invisible merge, and the earthly and otherworldly collide. I find this term apt, for when I saw the entities come into being in the artist's studio, I felt them incorporate the energies of the beings' crania, the various materials that comprise their bodies, as well as Durham's and his coworkers' creative labor. Further, when I attended the exhibition of *God's Children, God's Poems* at Zurich's contemporary art museum, I encountered a dynamic, interactive space with excited viewers, people who crouched near or looked up at Durham's assemblages, discussing what they experienced with their companions and strangers. The artists' skull creatures, made from what many people take to be resolutely dead matter, seemed somehow alive and affecting, poised between two realms in an animated space that animated others.

What does it mean to take seriously Durham's statement that he made spirit animals? First, respect for those who know spirit in what many take to be inanimate. Foremost, indigenous people the world over who know life in places, inert matter, and phenomena, as well as in creatures and plants. Anishinaabe and Haudenosaunee scholar Vanessa Watts describes indigenous Place-Thought as thinking and knowing by place and all entities within it, a collective of societies that negotiate responsibilities for coexisting well (2013, 21). Relationship with being considered dead in scientific terms shapes some forms of spiritual faith also, such as Shinto followers in Japan who honor stones and Neapolitan Catholics who care for human skulls as intercessors with the divine (Chavez 2011; Seymour 2018). For people who find it difficult to experience life in what they believe to be dead, another avenue exists for encountering spirit in *God's Children, God's Poems*. This path is possible through a willingness to embrace fiction and attend to its work, which, among other things, brings us into another world. In this case, once there, rather than suspend disbelief, believe that which is encountered to be true. Then, to see this belief not as matter of fact – something taken for granted as objective truth – but as the fact of the matter, what the very stuff of this world does when marshaled to shape conviction. Instead of received wisdom, such fiction creates new understanding. Durham's spirit animals, whether conceived as literally or figuratively alive, can open peoples' eyes to a different domain with different possibilities.

Skulls in and as Creation

Animal skulls have a long history in human creation. The oldest visually enhanced skull from North America to date is the "Cooper Skull," a crushed cranium of a now-extinct bison, painted with a red zigzag pattern over 10,500 years ago (Time Team 2012). Found in today's Oklahoma, it testifies to American Indians' extremely long and enduring relationship with the bison and its bones, the skull of which is iconic in Native art past and current. Today, Cannupa Hanska Luger, of Mandan, Hidatsa, Arikara, Lakota, and European descents, produces ceramic buffalo skull pieces, as well as installations with them that include animal bones, and does so to affirm American Indian history and culture, as well as critique how both are deeply scarred by colonialism up to the present ("Installation" n.d.). Bovine skulls also appear in prehistoric Eurasian art: plastered and sometimes painted bull skulls were set into main rooms in the 7500–5700 BCE Çatalhöyük settlement in today's Turkey (German n.d.). Bovine skulls occur too in art forms foundational for Western architecture and art: they are represented in Doric entablatures and sometimes Ionic and Corinthian friezes, where they likely refer to ancient Greek and Roman animal sacrifices (Loth 2013). Bovine and other animal skulls feature in some contemporary Euro-American art too. Sherrie Levine has produced glittering, mounted cast bronze steer and deer skulls, which signify the value that accrues to hunting trophies as well as to Georgia O'Keeffe's paintings of floating animal skulls (Hammer Museum 2017). These well-known paintings are emblems of American art and O'Keeffe produced many after settling in New Mexico where she encountered animal skulls in the desert and came to know several local American Indians. In nineteenth-century American Western art, the Indian and bison functioned as symbols of the supposedly dead Native culture upon which the American West was built (Coen 1973, 83–94). In O'Keeffe's painting of animal skulls and the visual culture of the American West it has helped spawn, the American also eclipses the Indian with the animal skull serving as sign of a US individual's "native" Southwestern identity.

Within the broad Western tradition of display, animal skulls and bones are more readily associated with science rather than art since countless specimens crowd cabinets and cases in natural history collections. Frequently brought back to Europe from fifteenth- through twentieth-century colonizing missions in Africa, the Americas, Asia, and the Pacific, these skeletons and bones were often accompanied by those of indigenous peoples (Shariatmadari 2018), creations produced by these peoples, as well as botanical, mineral, and sometimes living animal specimens, including humans (Çelik and Kinney 1990). First admired by learned collectors in Western royal collections, curiosity cabinets of the seventeenth century, and scientific compendia of the eighteenth century, all such inert items – including human remains – were ultimately viewed by the public in museums and universal expositions of the nineteenth and twentieth centuries (MacKenzie 2009). In Europe and America, indigenous creations were singled out as ethnographic objects within natural history collections when linked to anthropological study. Beginning in the nineteenth century, they were also viewed as art objects in the context of Primitivism: Westerners' use of "primitive" (i.e. not Western) creations as source material for experimental representation in art and subjectivity, notably Paul Gauguin's appropriation of Peruvian Indian and Pacific peoples' cultural forms to style himself a modern "savage" free of bourgeois repression. Damien Hirst's use of preserved and sometimes sliced animals showcased in glass vitrines, as well as his diamond-studded human skull, are perhaps the most famous instances of a contemporary artist indexing Westerners' past and continued fascination with animal remains within the mingled contexts of scientific and artistic display cultures. Hirst's creation of a jeweled human skull also points to two European traditions: the religious reliquary that honors saints' preserved remains, and the human skull as *memento mori* from the Classical period forward. The canonical European avant-garde artist Picasso, whose visual experiments are greatly indebted to his study of African and Pacific arts, during World War II transmuted the *memento mori* human skull into that of a bull, in part a means to communicate his Spanish identity by pointing toward bullfighting. Durham's animal skull works therefore exist in very potent contexts: histories of respectful and empowering interactions among living and dead animals on the one hand, and the complete opposite on the other. Durham's *God's Children, God's Poems* suggests ways to orient oneself toward the former.

Creating with, Creating alongside: Care

In March 2017, I went to the Berlin studio where Durham made the animal sculptures of *God's Children, God's Poems* with the help of his studio manager and chief assistant Kai-Morten Vollmer and assistant William Nicholson. Photographer Haley Floyd and videographer Kevin Pohle accompanied me to Durham's workspace in order to create visual reckonings of their experiences to share with me. Our visit coincided with that of art historian and Indigenous Studies scholar Richard William Hill, who came to Durham's studio to begin work on his essay for the *God's Children, God's Poems* exhibition catalogue. Floyd, Pohle, and I therefore entered a space brimming with the energy of inter-connected creative work, to which we ended up contributing through simple acts of sorting and preparing materials for use.

Prior to my Berlin trip, Durham and I exchanged letters via email in which we shared our experiences of and thoughts about animal-human relations. We reflected on our encounters with wild and domestic creatures, and with ideas about and practices with animals in husbandry, science, art, and entertainment. In these discussions, Durham rejected anthropocentrism, favoring instead human connections with animals that respect difference and respond to need. We had an exchange about lizards that I found particularly illuminating in this regard. After I told him a story about an anole outside my office window giving me "dirty looks," he told me about making drinking cups for anoles as a young boy (Jimmie Durham, e-mail message to the author, February 25, 2017). While my tale turned a creature into a little person focused on me, in Durham's account, lizards are beings in and of themselves that he succors. He offered nourishment to which they responded, whereas in my story, the anole was a prop for my conceit. When I looked at the lizard who looked at me, I projected onto the animal; I did not consider how something might pass between us that marked both difference and connection.

In further exchanges with Durham, I saw that the latter dynamic characterizes all of his relationships with animals. While dining and strolling with him and others in Zurich upon the occasion of *God's Children, God's Poems'* opening, I watched him happily feed birds with crumbs of bread from his meal and mine. While doing so, Durham recalled his former studio in Berlin's Grunewald Forest, where he spent every day enjoying a repast with animal neighbors. With these experiences and the artist's tale of offering water to lizards in mind, I came to see that all of Durham's interactions with animals involve care. And reflecting on my experience in the Berlin studio where the creatures for *God's Children, God's Poems* came into being, I saw that this was true of Durham's interactions there with animal skulls, other materials, his colleagues, mine, and me. All distinct, all came together with Durham's animal spirits.

As I sat next to Durham at his studio worktable, I saw him use great sensitivity while enlivening a bear skull (Figure 4.1).

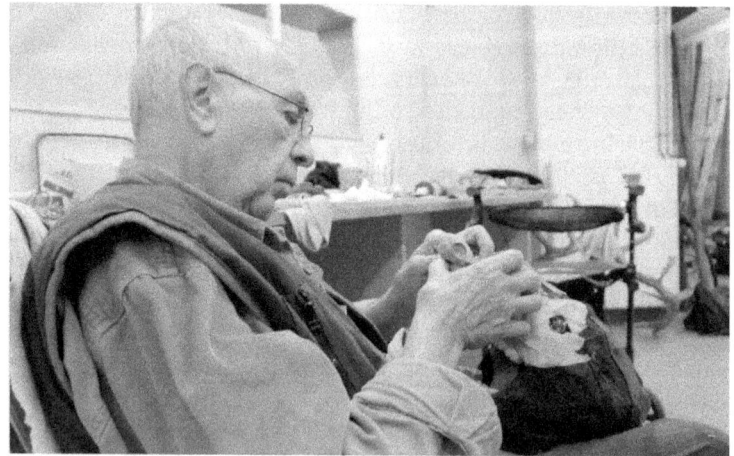

Figure 4.1 Jimmie Durham working on a bear skull in his Berlin studio, March 2017, video still, Kevin Pohle.

The skull frightened me at first, for its powerful jaws with large, sharp teeth appeared even in death ready to puncture, crush, and shred skin, muscle, and bone. However, my anxious response softened as I watched Durham affix strips of leather to the top of the bear skull and pieces of Murano glass along its jawline. Observing Durham respond to the shape, feel, and look of the skull with concentration and care, I started to find the bear head inviting as well as fearsome, and sought respectful distance from it along with quiet connection. Durham accounts for such twinned impulses in his 1992 essay "Approach in Love and Fear." In this text, he maintains that love overrides fear of others to produce union, initially to propagate, but ultimately to form caring bonds with everything (1993, 229–30). In his text for the *God's Children, God's Poems* catalogue, Durham says that such love comes with the responsibility to treat animals as brethren who live with rather than for us (2017, 12).

Love is an experience many individuals have with pets and other tame animals, and scores of people would associate with their exposure to wild animals out of doors and in photographs, films, and zoos. These different types of love, one born of actual relations and the other passion from afar, point to varied incarnations of feelings and actions that involve others, animal and otherwise. Love twinned with the responsibility Durham calls for requires people to negotiate tensions around care about and for others: to ask what and how we give and take, and why and where does selflessness and self-interest enter into the equation. These are critical questions for Europeans and their descendants who colonized parts of the world now dying, places where indigenous peoples' relationships with animals and other entities were and remain mutually sustaining. Culture and media theorist Heather Davis and Métis social anthropologist Zoe Todd show that colonization, and resistance to it, is at the very root of the Anthropocene.

> … Indigenous peoples contended with the end of their worlds, and continue to work to foster and tend to strong relationships to humans, other-than-humans, and land today. This Indigenous resistance in the face of apocalypse, and the renewal and resurgence of Indigenous communities in spite of world-ending violence is something that Euro-Western thinkers should heed as we contend with the implications of the Imperial forces that set in motion the seismic upheaval of worlds back in 1492.
>
> (2017, 773)

Some Western thinkers now mine their own philosophical inheritance for strands of thought and action concerning caring interrelationships and do so to challenge ongoing Western praxis that has won out but must no longer: imperatives to objectify, possess, use up, and destroy. Philosopher María Puig de la Bellacasa has produced a complex, sensitive, and situated understanding of care as generative bonds among others that nourish the life-sustaining web our shared world can be. Puig de la Bellacasa's vision, which is grounded in touch as well as sight, makes room for all entities, both those traditionally understood to be alive and also dead. Touch is crucial for her since literally and figuratively touching others entails closer proximity than seeing, and therefore intimacy accompanied by vulnerability. Such intensity allows her to address the stakes humans have in gain and loss, and to consider how we can care about, for, and with the entities we live among to seek "ways of living together as well as possible" (2017, Introduction).

Like Puig de la Bellacasa, Durham in *God's Children, God's Poems* makes no prescriptive claims for what "nonexploitive forms of togetherness" might entail (ibid.). However, his physical interactions with the bear head that I observed in his studio, and the felt sensations the head solicits, challenge drives to objectify creation. Touch is a key here: it appears in virtually all artworks, and many artists, famously van Gogh, foreground the tactile by making the corporeal gestures that formed their pieces evident. Although those who see the animals of *God's Children, God's Poems* cannot touch them, Durham has made the creatures a virtual haptic experience: the sculptures' highly textured materials and evident means of construction invite connection. Puig de la Bellacasa's understanding of touch in care suggests how Durham's studio practices work toward making connection. He involved his assistants, his colleague Hill, and my colleagues and myself in physical creative work, and he involves his audience in bodily experience of his animal sculptures. In his catalogue essay for *God's Children, God's Poems*, Durham says that his pieces "are made socially for us – for me and for anyone else who might see them" (2017, 11). He removes himself as the sole animating force of creation and understanding, shaping instead relations through which physical experience and meaning arise together with the skull sculptures and the people who encounter them with one another.

Presences and Entrainment

While Durham created his animals, his studio brimmed with items for making that he constantly replenished – natural and manmade found objects, collected scraps, harvested detritus, gifted castoffs, and purchased goods. Boxes with ethically sourced animal skulls arrived to join the mix of these things gathered in piles, stacks, and arrangements, and the crania ended up tucked into corners, placed on shelves, and laid out on the floor. The skulls became a part of a shifting mass of materials considered, handled, and augmented by creators, standing out amidst the array because of how powerfully they evoked both life and death. As Durham enhanced the skulls with other materials, also dead in the traditional sense, the combinations appeared increasingly animate. Shimmering paint evoked temperature, glowing glass transmitted energy, spiraling shells implied motion, and textured wood communicated strength. Dead and alive intermingled in artistic creation.

Haley Floyd's photographs of the skulls capture these oscillations between death and life, as well as the sense of presence that adheres to the skulls whether worked upon or not. She used a 4 × 5 camera to make her images, which involved a close interaction with her apparatus, the crania, and the setting she devised for them. Since the 4 × 5 camera is large, requires a hood, and uses individual film sheets, and because Durham gave Floyd permission to handle and arrange the skulls as she saw fit, she took a great deal of time and care to set up her shots. Because the 4 × 5 camera gives a photographer a lot of physical control over focus and perspective through manual adjustments, Floyd took additional time to consider and fine-tune the composition and qualities of her pictures. Her working process thus paralleled the physical and cognitive give and take that took place with Durham, his materials, and the skulls. Floyd's approach also involved the human interaction that occurred between Durham and those who assisted him: like him, she solicited and was offered feedback. Floyd not only recorded what she saw in Durham's studio, but she also participated in its life. She produced portraits of the crania, drawing on a genre in art that pays tribute to the life portrayed, creating black and white images of skulls that Durham had not yet altered, and color images of those skulls he had.

Portraits focus on subjects' faces, and Floyd did this by selecting plain backdrops that unobtrusively frame the skulls, which fill the picture plane so we can see their intrinsic nature, and how Durham responded to those he worked upon (Figure 4.2).

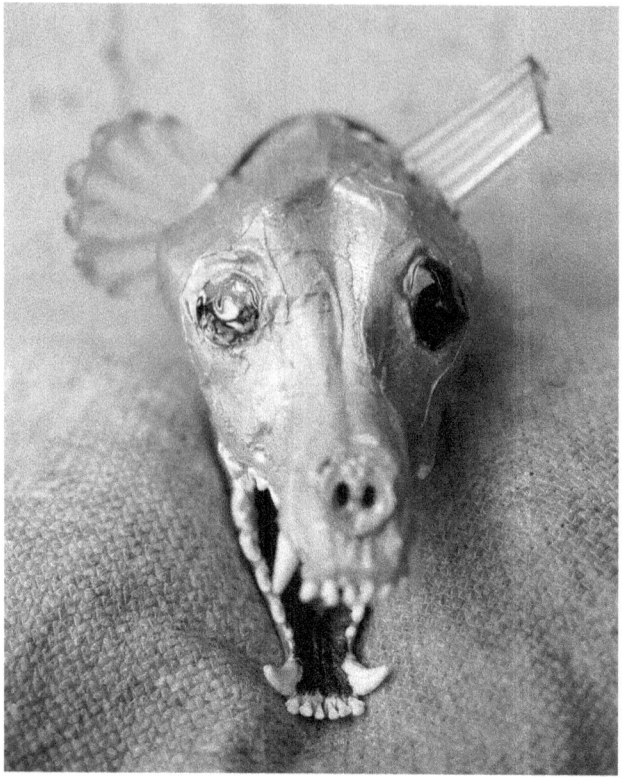

Figure 4.2 Haley Floyd, *Jimmie Durham's Great Dane Skull*, 2017, photograph, collection of the artist.

Philosopher Emanuel Levinas argues that when we see and truly
pay attention to an individual's face, we cannot turn whom we view
into a site of projection or a thing for use (1969, 79–81). Ethnogra-
pher Deborah Bird Rose extends Levinas' focus on the human face
to include that of the animal, and this expansion shifts experience
of relations into a matrix of regard in which all being can matter
(2011, chap. 3). Floyd's portraits of Durham's animal skulls, like the
skulls themselves, participate in Rose's vision of honoring varied
others' vital integrity. Floyd's photographs give us access to creatures by showing us their faces, how we might view them through
Durham's eyes and handiwork, along with her own.

This is a layered experience of regard in both the sense of looking
and valuing. Viewers are drawn to distinctions and made aware of

interactions in the photographs: differences among the skulls both altered and not, as well as among representational strategies Durham and Floyd employed. Floyd's portraits reveal the stark beauty of the skulls before they were enlivened as well as the dynamic energy they radiate after Durham enhanced them, and connection attends both encounters. Empty eye sockets and those with eyes of glass, shell, or other materials draw viewers into relation with the skulls along with the artists who touched and gazed upon the crania to give us their sense of connection with the animal heads. We become acutely aware of relation with both presence and absence: those of the artists and the animals that are "there" and not. This experience orients us toward Durham's understanding of *God's Children, God's Poems* as "spirit animals," and guides my understanding of the crania as presences. Philosopher Amélie Oksenberg Rorty defines a presence as an existence that does not seek to control action or compel feeling (1976, 301–23). She argues instead that presences enable a face-to-face exchange that challenges projection onto another being. Presences thus resonate with Bird's amplification of Levinas' understanding of mutual regard: encounters that honor difference as and with integrity. The animal skulls with which Durham creates are not ghosts that incite through haunting, but instead presences that engage on equal footing and without demands.

Durham's and Richard Hill's essays for the *God's Children, God's Poems* catalogue and one of Kevin Pohle's videos of Durham working on an animal assemblage focus on processes of give and take in creation: perceptive views of Durham's interactions with his materials and the life at their interstices. Durham's exhibition essay in conjunction with novelist and essayist Ursula K. Le Guin's writing on human-animal relations provides a framework to relate these views to one another: story. Like Le Guin, Durham favors conversational storytelling in writing, and thinking with her in mind about what he commits to the page and communicates while filmed yields insight into the sort of recognition and connection his animal spirits enable.

Le Guin writes stories about what she calls animal presences, maintaining that story is the vehicle through which we can be *with* animals rather than have them be *for* us, which she implies happens often in conventional prose that takes animals as objects of study or use. Le Guin shows that the oral and written stories of myth, fable, children's literature, and fantasy fiction produce sites where being of all sorts comes together in worlds that parallel our own, but that are enriched by exchanges among different entities, both alive and dead. Le Guin maintains that animal presences cannot populate those arenas in which human control is privileged (1990, 7–12). To enact this point, she glides from tight, descriptive prose to fluid, evocative poetry, all the while maintaining a conversational stance as she draws us into an imaginative realm. She thereby positions herself at our side, welcoming us into a space of connection with her and with animal presences alive with her creative energy.

Durham's essay for *God's Children, God's Poems* operates in this manner too, speaking of distance and proximity among humans and animals, and suggesting how we might make our relations with our animal brethren more respectful. He recounts a story of meeting in a field a large, black stallion that thwarted his attempt at friendship: Durham moved toward the horse to touch him, but the creature ran away with speed and grandeur that thrilled the artist. This tale sets the stage for Durham's subsequent meditations on human-animal relations. He sees that we often come to animals wanting something of them, but when they are free, their terms matter and may not include us – beyond an experience of their beauty in independence. When animals do enter into a direct relationship with us, Durham maintains that we have a duty to care about and for them as we would with our closest human companions (2017, 12).

This ethos pervades Durham tribute to the large animals of Europe in *God's Children, God's Poems*, both at the level of the beings' creation and their display. Hill's exhibition catalogue essay and Pohle's videos capture Durham's studio practice and reveal an artist dedicated to each material he uses, a commitment that extends beyond appreciation for how something can be employed to how *it* calls to be incorporated. Hill recounts Durham's intense engagement with the leather, glass, pipe, and other items that comprise his animals, a sort of mental and physical dialogue that Pohle explores in video (see Figure 4.1).

Hill's essay describes the many and varied activities and materials that make Durham's skull assemblages come into being. Hill details the full range of items the artist employed, the specific ways Durham combined and affixed materials, and the means by which he obtained things he used. Hill accompanied Durham to a used clothing store, a scrapyard, as well as a DIY home and garden center, and in his essay recounts watching the artist recognize parts of animal bodies in items he saw and touched. Hill also describes processes that Durham came up with to affix material to animal skulls, painting a verbal picture of the soaking, gluing, placing, stretching, and smoothing gestures Durham performed to affix chamois to bone. Additionally, Hill depicts the vivid qualities of the items Durham used, and how they became further animated with the artist's work.

When I arrive, the enormous Shire Horse skull has already been given the foundation of a neck in the form of a heavy wooden plank, supplemented by sections of unmilled wood. It has ears made of wood and a thin, bright, and shiny sheet of copper that has been crumpled up and placed into the nose cavity, where it suggests to me the horse's steaming breath, a sign, perhaps, of its life force.

(2017, 75)

Pohle's videos visually demonstrate how Durham achieved such animated effects. Like Hill, Pohle captures the dynamic relationships in the artist's studio that produced the skull assemblages: his roving video camera gives distant and close views of activities and things. Pohle's videos depict the large scale and great depth of the *God's Children, God's Poems* project as a whole, for they show the intense amount of work and complexity of processes that shaped skull assemblages as they moved through varied stages of becoming. In one video of Durham working on the brown bear skull, Pohle moves his video camera along with Durham's hands, documenting the precise and considered actions Durham took to affix material to the cranium. Viewers see that with gentle finger and fingernail pressure, the artist molded chamois to bone and to a piece of curled wood that became the bear's nose. In the video, the skin and bone of man and animal seem to move together in the making. Through Hill's words and Pohle's images, we therefore see glimpses of Durham acknowledging materials' properties and how they communicate their best realization in assembled being.

Le Guin maintains that such a connection entails what physicists call entrainment: "mutual phase locking," whereby entities come into sync with one another. This is no rote reflection, but instead an exchange through which difference finds a shared rhythm: a point of contact as attunement (2012, "Telling is Listening"). Entrainment not only describes Durham's relationship with his materials and how he creates with them, but also suggests how we can experience *God's Children, God's Poems*. Durham had an entire, large, well-lit gallery in which to display his animal assemblages in Zurich, and positioned each very deliberately to initiate varied connections among the creatures, the spaces they inhabited, and the viewers who encountered them. Durham's configurations did

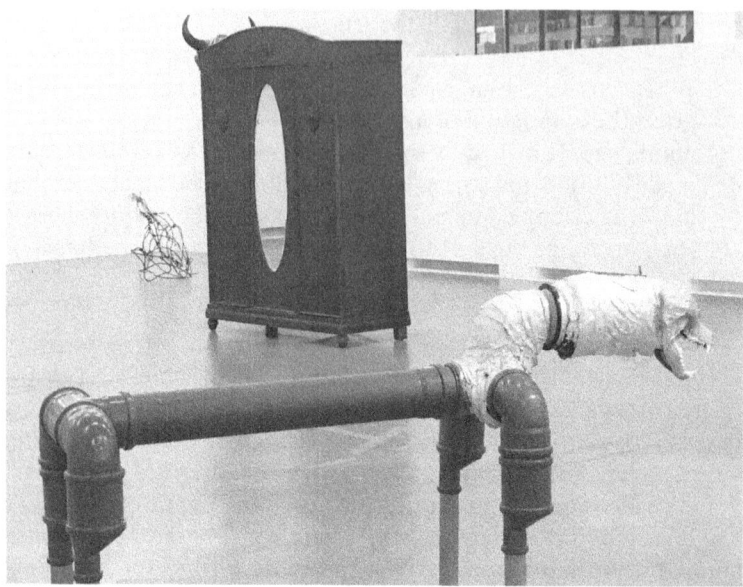

Figure 4.3 Jimmie Durham, *Eurasian Lynx*, 2017, lynx skull, cotton, leather, Murano glass, metal, wire, plastic, 136 × 61 × 70 cm, collection of the artist; *Bison/Wisent*, 2017, European bison skull, wooden armoire, glass, steel, car paint (chameleon), 203 × 72 × 187 cm, collection of the artist; *Great Dane*, 2017, dog skull, Murano glass, black walnut shell, cotton, PE-pipes, steel, rubber, acrylic paint, 170 × 50 × 122 cm, collection of the artist (view, Migros Museum für Gegenwartskunst, Zurich, 2017).

not force specific relationships, but clearly invited sites of sensation and paths of inquiry for museum visitors to explore (Figure 4.3).

Upon entering the gallery, each person immediately confronted a squat, fierce boar sculpture; when occupying the far left section of the space, each individual encountered a tightly coiled, springing lynx work, and when traveling across the middle of the exhibition, each visitor moved past the towering Shire horse assemblage. The skulls of the animal pieces compelled viewers' attention since the bony crania evoke sharp discomfort with death, while the radiant materials that animate the heads conjure the enduring lives of the creatures and all that made them. In situ, *God's Children, God's Poems* thereby called upon those who saw the show to engage the range of experiences one might feel, think, and imagine in the animal spirits' presences. For some, this entailed entrainment, finding a rhythm that led to specific artworks that resonated in some way, and on some level. I saw this as I watched people experience Durham's skull assemblages, and was struck by how they were transfixed by particular pieces. One group of friends kept coming back to the boar; a woman remained with the ibex much longer than any other creature; a boy moved back and forth among different deer; and a family stood with the bear several times discussing different aspects of it on each occasion.

Agencement

Durham and philosopher Vinciane Despret each explore relationships between presence and absence: how we experience understanding when working with what we believe we have, and what we may discover when working with what we do not – but may come into being alongside us. Durham and Despret pursue similar paths, and offer rich possibilities for conceiving community that welcomes and sustains. Following the trajectories they trace helps me articulate my understanding of the animal spirits Durham shares with viewers, and their shared spirit of connection.

In his *God's Children, God's Poems* exhibition catalogue essay, Durham answers an imagined question about what an audience is to "get" from his work. He suggests that we cannot know in advance because experience of his assemblages unfolds in particular relations in specific moments (2017, 11). Durham's statement parallels a manner of being that Despret calls *agencement*: making and knowing formed by give-and-take among all elements of creation as it becomes and is received. Rather than locate agency and outcome in any one life, Despret maintains that within situated relationships among organic and inorganic entities, each affects one another by engaging interest, with results that continue to create more interactions and happenings (2013, 44). From this perspective, what we typically think of as singularity – subject, object, beginning, end – opens into multiplicity, becoming through which particular things happen at a given time. Such an expanded notion of involvement recognizes the power typically unacknowledged others (alive and dead in the traditional sense), have to inform recognized power: institutions and persons that determine where value lies and how it accrues, no matter who or what suffers. Within Despret's framework, those empowered in one context might ask what it is to be so in the worldview and circumstances they know, and how both might shift and expand were they to ask how what they live among contributes to other realities.

Despret elucidates the modality she advocates primarily by look-ing at animal science, but also by investigating beliefs about death. With respect to the former, she notes that ethologists often ask ques-tions about animals with answers already in mind, creating experi-ments that deliver anticipated results to meet established objectives. Frequently, scientists do the knowing, animals are the known, and both can be hurt in the process, as when researchers fret over the fate of aging apes who cease to serve their purpose. An equally impov-erished dynamic operates in accepted notions of death in Western culture today since the natural and social sciences define death as finitude, maintain that the dead and their mourners no longer share life, and declare that loss is to be mastered and assuaged.

Despret shows that methods of inquiry that make animals, the dead, and humans equal and respected partners yield information and ideas that can create marvelous, enriching connections. She demonstrates this with her answer to the question "Do chimpanzees experience mourning?" a query that went viral on the internet when *National Geo-graphic* posted a photograph of the animals gathered quietly around the corpse of one of their elders. Noting that normative responses to mourning among humans today stress accepting that the dead are for-ever gone, and that many who wondered about the chimpanzees with their dead considered this may be the case for the apes as well, Despret states that there is no demonstrable reason for chimpanzees to think about this. She maintains that we have every reason to question *our* understanding of and reactions to death. Her vantage point permits us to recognize that human mourning is historical and inculcated: in much of the West at present, experience of the dead as real among the living is only possible in imagination rather than truth. For Despret, the answer to the question "Do chimpanzees experience mourning?" is a response many would not have anticipated: perhaps we might re-consider what we think is certain about life and death wherever they occur – with animals, with humans, and I would add here, art (2016, "V for Versions"). As with Despret, Durham creates anew our rela-tionships with animals and death. With *God's Children, God's Poems*, we see animal presences freed from the prisons we in the West often place them in: zoo and lab cages for the living; taxidermy displays and museum dioramas for the dead; and farm and slaughterhouse factories for those we kill. Arrayed freely in space oriented toward one another and us, Durham's animal skulls with bodies challenge these scenarios. As spirits, they exist at the place where life and death meet, the visible and invisible merge, and the earthly and otherworldly collide.

This is especially true for the spirit animal that seems to en-gage viewers least, and which appears most dead: the wisent, or

European bison. Durham's wisent is subdued in color, weighty in form, and in the Zurich exhibition faced a window, appearing to look beyond the space it inhabited. The wisent's body is an old, tall, wooden wardrobe, and the creature's skull sits at the top of the piece of furniture, on one of its narrow sides. Durham minimally enhanced the cranium with gray, iridescent paint, and filled one eye socket with a piece of broken glass, and the other, a camera lens. When encountered, the creature seems away and removed – until we contemplate our own image in the full-length mirror on a wide expanse of the wardrobe (Figure 4.4).

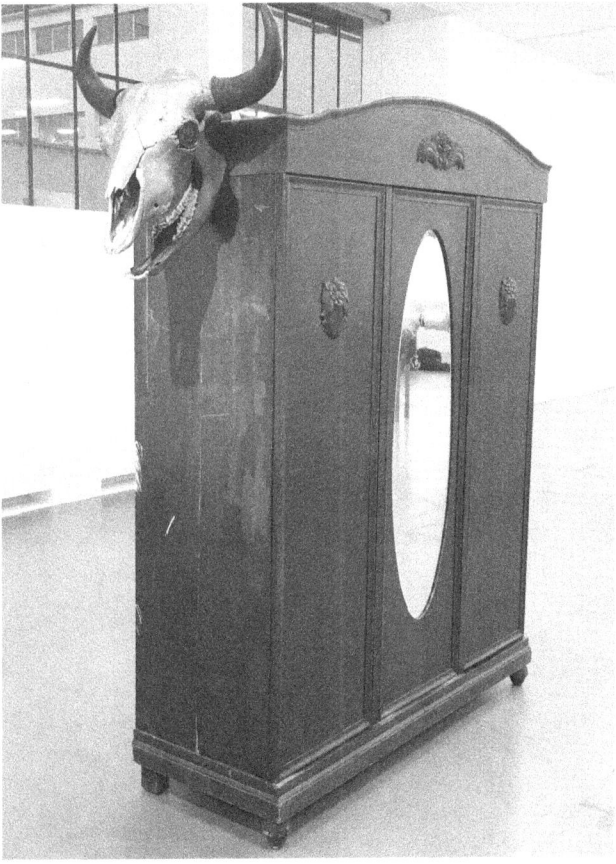

Figure 4.4 Jimmie Durham, *Bison/Wisent*, 2017, European bison skull, wooden armoire, glass, steel, car paint (chameleon), 203 × 72 × 187 cm, collection of the artist (view, Migros Museum für Gegenwartskunst, Zurich, 2017).

Positioned at the wisent's side, we see ourselves reflected within its body. This is an invitation that issues from the wisent via Durham: together, both ask us to reflect on our relationship to an animal that is almost extinct, and a death that is animated by everything and everybody – including our own body – who made and continues to make the animal spirit. Do we see ourselves in loss? In gain? In both? In 1982, Durham encouraged us to see his baby buffalo skull work as bridging loss and gain. He does so once more with the European buffalo skull, less overtly, but in a more embodied manner. The wisent has a body and we must use ours to experience the creature fully: we look up and walk around it to determine where we stand in relation to it, both physically and ethically. As we orient ourselves, specific questions may arise: Where do we fit in with the demise of the wisent and other species? What does the wisent communicate in death? What does it communicate as an artwork animated by those who created with it?

I think Durham's animal skull assemblages made in tandem with his materials and fellows embody creative and intellectual community as respectful interrelationships among animals, humans, things, and places. Death and loss are real conditions of the Anthropocene; *God's Children, God's Poems* demonstrate that they needn't signal an end. The skull assemblages are a tribute to Europe's animals as well as to the wider world: recognition that we may have the capacity to make something better rather than further destroy. Yorick's skull in Hamlet communicates absolute loss. In *God's Children, God's Poems*, skulls from the largest creatures of Europe, together with creation as making and receiving, invite us to think otherwise. Maybe we can reorient our relationships to animals to help them thrive. Perhaps we can see that presence remains in death and that it asks us to consider what we enable and what we abandon – and what this means for all of creation.

References

Çelik, Zeynep and Leila Kinney. 1990. "Ethnography and Exhibitionism at the Expositions Universelles." *Assemblage* 13 (December): 34–59. https://doi.org/10.2307/3171106.

Chavez, Amy. 2011. "On Rock Worship and the Shinto Gods." *Japan Times*, July 9, 2011. https://www.japantimes.co.jp/community/2011/07/09/our-lives/on-rock-worship-and-the-shinto-gods/#.XmZmzpVKjcs.

Coen, Rena N. 1973. "The Last of the Buffalo." *The American Art Journal* 5, no. 2 (November): 83–94. https://doi.org/10.2307/1593957.

Davis, Heather and Zoe Todd. 2017. "On the Importance of a Date, or Decolonizing the Anthropocene." *ACME* 16, no. 4: 761–80.

Despret, Vinciane. 2013. "From Secret Agents to Interagency." *History and Theory* 52, no. 4 (December): 29–44. https://doi.org/10.1111/hith.10686.

———. 2016. *What Would Animals Say If We Asked the Right Questions?* Translated by Brett Buchanan. Minneapolis: University of Minnesota Press. Kindle. https://doi.org/10.5749/minnesota/9780816692378.001.0001.

Durham, Jimmie. 1993. "Approach in Love and Fear." In *A Certain Lack of Coherence: Writings on Art and Cultural Politics*, edited by Jean Fisher, 229–30. London: Kala Press.

———. 2017. "Europe." In *God's Children, God's Poems*, edited by Heike Munder, 11–13. Zurich: Migros Museum für Gegenwartskunst and JRP|Ringier.

German, Senta. n.d. "Çatalhöyük." Khan Academy. Accessed January 15, 2020. https://www.khanacademy.org/humanities/prehistoric-art/neolithic-art/a/atalhyk.

Hammer Museum. 2017. "Steer Skull, Horned." Take It or Leave It: Institution, Image, Ideology Digital Archive. https://hammer.ucla.edu/take-it-or-leave-it/art/steer-skull-horned.

Hanska, Cannupa. n.d. "Installation." Accessed January 15, 2020. http://www.cannupahanska.com/installation-1.

Hill, Richard William. 2017. "Nine Days Living amongst the Very Large Animals of Europe." In *God's Children, God's Poems*, edited by Heike Munder, 71–81. Zurich: Migros Museum für Gegenwartskunst and JRP|Ringier.

Le Guin, Ursula K. 1990. *Buffalo Gals and Other Animal Presences*. New York: Penguin Books.

———. 2012. *The Wave in the Mind: Talks and Essays on the Writer, the Reader, and the Imagination*. Boston, MA: Shambhala Press. Kindle.

Levinas, Emmanuel. 1969. *Totality and Infinity: An Essay on Exteriority*. Translated by Alphonso Lingis. Pittsburgh, PA: Duquesne University Press.

Loth, Calder. 2013. "Bucrania: Classical Comments." The Institute of Classical Architecture & Art website. https://www.classicist.org/articles/classical-comments-bucrania/.

MacKenzie, John M. 2009. *Museums and Empire: Natural History, Human Cultures and Colonial Identities*. Manchester: Manchester University Press.

Pesticides Action Network. 2017. "Over 300 Food and Farm Groups Urge Jeff Sessions to Oppose Agricultural Mega-mergers." http://www.panna.org/press-release/over-300-food-and-farm-groups-urge-jeff-sessions-oppose-agricultural-mega-mergers.

Puig de la Bellacasa, María. 2017. *Matters of Care: Speculative Ethics in More Than Human Worlds*. Minneapolis: University of Minnesota Press. Kindle.

Rorty, Amélie Oksenberg. 1976. "A Literary Postscript: Persons, Selves, Individuals." In *The Identity of Persons*, edited by Amélie Oksenberg Rorty, 301–24. Berkeley: University of California Press.

Rose, Deborah Bird. 2011. *Wild Dog Dreaming: Love and Extinction*. Charlottesville and London: University of Virginia Press. Kindle edition.

Seymour, Sophia. 2018. "Naples' Fontanelle Cemetery: Skulls and Silence Beneath the Busy City Streets." *The Guardian*, January 12, 2018. https://www.theguardian.com/travel/2018/jan/12/naples-cemetery-delle-fontanelle-italy-skulls.

Shariatmadari, David. 2018. "'They're Not Property': The People Who Want Their Ancestors Back from British Museums." *The Guardian*, April 23, 2018. https://www.theguardian.com/culture/2019/apr/23/theyre-not-property-the-people-who-want-their-ancestors-back-from-british-museums.

Time Team. 2012. "Red Lightning Strikes Twice." http://www.pbs.org/time-team/explore-the-sites/bones-badger-hole/cooper-skull/.

Watts, Vanessa. 2013. "Indigenous Place-Thought & Agency amongst Humans and Non-humans (First Woman and Sky Woman Go on a European World Tour!)." *Decolonization: Indigeneity, Education & Society* 2, no. 1: 20–34.

World Animal Protection. n.d. "Animal Protection Index: Switzerland." Accessed January 1, 2020. https://api.worldanimalprotection.org/country/switzerland.

Conclusion – Humanity Is Not a Completed Project

In Room Four dedicated to glass in Alves and Durham's *The Middle Earth*, the artists provided a statement about glass' properties. They noted that it is one of five states of material: solid, liquid, gas, dark matter, and glass. We typically experience glass as a solid although we know that it is molten too before cooling. However, glass does not in fact solidify, but appears to because it is in "a state of flow slower than the expansion of the universe" (2018; Queen Mary, University of London 2011). This is a surprising and powerful condition that suggests things need not be "either/or." They can be "and." It is perhaps difficult to understand how a physical entity can be two – maybe more – things at once. We know that people can have different identities and different perspectives on matters; it is challenging for many to see that, for example, matter can be inanimate in one sense and animate in another. The lifeways of indigenous peoples and religious experience for numerous individuals confirm this condition, and today scholars who write about materialism and vitalism in new ways work with this understanding too (Coole and Frost 2010; de la Cadena and Blaser 2018). Queer of Color, Feminist, and Disability Studies linguist Mel Y. Chen employs the term "animacy" to describe what in life and current academic theory undoes "stubborn binary systems of difference, including dynamism/stasis, life/death, subject/object, speech/nonspeech, human/animal, natural body/cyborg" (2012, 3).

That matter, and what matters, can be separate as well as conjoined is a critical dimension of Durham's practice. Analyzing the artist's work in tandem with the ideas of varied thinkers, I've argued that his *Something… Perhaps a Fugue or an Elegy*, two *presepi*, *The Middle Earth* with Maria Thereza Alves, and *God's Children, God's Poems* embody and communicate connection in difference, value in detritus, and renewal in loss. Seeing such embeddedness in Durham's art requires reorientation. For example, to see value in detritus is to find something previously dismissed important and to alter one's relationship to it. Before I engaged Durham's work, I thought broken glass was junk to throw away or recycle. Now, I see it as a unique form of matter neither solid nor liquid that can help bring to life an entity that hails me, such as a bear skull vivified with Murano glass on its way to becoming one of *God's Children* – a being that both worries and delights me.

One of Durham's very recent assemblages with glass especially captures this type of reorientation toward duality: his 2019 *Blue Flower*, a light blue Murano glass flower from a broken chandelier entwined with and suspended by rusted thick, steel wire. Murano glass chandeliers have been precious markers of wealth since the seventeenth century (Grinberg 2013) and heavy-gauge metal wire has been a key material in industry since the nineteenth century (The Editors of Encyclopaedia Britannica 2019). Thus, the "high" and "low" fuse in *Blue Flower*. This is also true for the sacred and profane: Durham's assemblage made from very secular materials appeared in one of Naples' most esteemed Catholic sites. Gifted by the artist to Naples' Pio Monte della Misericordia Church for its contemporary art collection program, *Blue Flower* hung during the early months of 2020 in the chapel that houses one of the city's greatest artworks: Michelangelo Merisi da Caravaggio's 1607 *The Seven Acts of Mercy*. Caravaggio's art is itself both every day and extraordinary, combining humble and divine characters, as well as straightforward and unearthly effects.

Writing to art historian and curator Mario Codognato, who organized the exhibition of contemporary art the Pio Monte della Misericordia Church acquired in 2019, Durham pointed to duality in *Blue Flower* beyond material use and art historical reference: he said that he named *Blue Flower* with the writer Novalis and an aspect of indigenous cosmology in mind (Jimmie Durham, email to author, December 6, 2019). The blue flower embodies the desired yet potentially impossible in German Romantic literature informed by Novalis' 1802 *Heinrich von Ofterdingen*, and Durham sees the blue flower as an emblem of hope in an Aztec worldview. For Novalis and subsequent creators he inspired, the blue flower points to a quest for fulfillment – spiritual, romantic, or otherwise – that doggedly continues despite seeming unattainability (Porter 1989, 16). For Aztecs, blue was precious: as turquoise and jade, it was great wealth, and as color, it marked the sustaining realms of water and daylight sky (Rossell 2005; Peterson and Terraciano 2019, 157–58). Aztecs also revered flowers as beloved earthly companions and religious offerings bound up in war and poetry in equal measure. As ferocity in death and joy in life for Aztecs (Damrosch 1991, 102–5), flowers conveyed experience as transience and transition.

With this Aztec sense of blue as sustenance and flowers as animacy in life/death, Durham's connection between the blue flower and hope enriches Novalis' image of possibly unrewarded striving. Hung above viewers like Caravaggio's *The Seven Acts of Mercy*, *Blue Flower* cannot be reached through physical contact, but as with the Baroque painting famed for depicting deep compassion, the assemblage can be felt through affective and cognitive connection. Through *Blue Flower,* we encounter striving for presence in absence as Novalis conceives it, but also sense that we are *amidst* presence in absence, as Aztecs may have known it.

My reading of Durham's flower parallels my understanding of his other recent artworks made in Europe that I have discussed in this book. I believe that *Something... Perhaps a Fugue or an Elegy*, Durham's two *presepi*, *The Middle Earth* with Maria Thereza Alves, and *God's Children, God's Poems* ask us to think about how and why we form the connections that we do – in our minds and then in our relations – and to question what this says about what we value and what this might lead to. I have made this argument in the context of a utopian vision that reflects my investment in hope as philosopher Ernst Bloch conceives it and anthropologist Hirokazu Miyazaki applies it. Bloch does not view utopia as an already conceived abstract state of affairs to be realized under the guidance of visionaries. Instead, he sees it as "a growing together of tendencies and latencies within the relationship between material reality and human intervention which are always full with potential but which cannot be realized because the material conditions for their realization is not yet complete" (Bloch and Ritter 1976, 10; Thompson 2013).

Miyazaki embraces Bloch's insistence on the "not-yet" and does so as a method informed by the work he observed within a group of Suvavou Fijians and their more than 100-year fight to gain compensation for the theft of their land. Miyazaki looks at the many different ways these people approached the colonial government and continue to approach the national government with their demands. Miyazaki sees that the Fijians' self-understanding is shaped by what is true (*dina*) and effective (*mana*), and observes that when one approach to reparation fails, another is built upon a shift in thinking about and acting upon what is deemed the true, right way (2004, 3). This becomes Miyazaki's method of hope: he learns from and creates with something passed that did not work to make something constructive in the present in view of a coming positive outcome. Through this method, he arrives at a conception of time, history, and politics that not only parallels those of his Suvavouan fellows, but also what he finds in Bloch: bits of the past reconceived can inform the now toward a better future (140).

People anxious about world flourishing today may wonder about what hope affords. Conversation across ideological lines, just politics, and climate repair seem beyond reach. The latter existential threat affects disadvantaged communities and poor nations first, but increasingly involves everyone and everything whatever naysayers claim. Some people may worry that their efforts to become "greener" amount to virtually nothing. Others may despair that those abused by corporate and government mismanagement and deceit will never get their due: for example, residents of Flint, Michigan have yet to get clean water after more than five years of protest even though almost 200 of their children suffer lead poisoning (Alfonsi 2020). Although Swedish climate activist Greta Thunberg inspires people to fight against the crippling effects of fossil fuel usage and other destructive human practices, whether or not change on the scale necessary to address growing species loss, environmental destruction, forced migrations, food insecurity, extreme weather events, and other catastrophes remains to be seen. As I finish this book, the Covid-19 pandemic rages and although the best of humanity is unfolding to address the crisis, so too is its worst: while health workers put their lives in danger to succor the ill, people hoard hand sanitizer and sell it for astronomical prices. In dire situations such as these, hope may seem wide-eyed or an excuse to dream rather than do.

In 2006, Durham created the short artwork statement *Humanity Is Not a Completed Project*. In an essay about it, he notes that cynicism is part of naivety that pretends to know the future, which, in fact, cannot be known. He observes that humans have existed for over a million years and only learned to write 6,000 years ago, which suggests "that we can and will change, and therefore that the actions of individuals can be effective" (2014, 367). Scholars in the Arts, Humanities, and Social Sciences scrutinize the terms "the individual" and "the human" because they are often universalized but are in fact typically specific to the experience of privileged, abled, heteronormative, white people, usually male but often female too. "The individual" and "the human" if not nuanced veil complex interrelationships among people, and also fail to communicate the ways in which humans make up webs of being with other entities.

Durham's work takes up these problematic dynamics. "Humanity" and "individuals" in his practice address responsibility humans as a species and individuals as humans have to think about how we exist with others whether sentient or not, in specific conditions of compatibility or opposition.

As I noted in my book introduction, Durham does not presuppose that what he puts forth is interesting or productive: "no" and disengagement can attend what he does. However, when connection in and through his art does arise, I experience it as a practice of hope: finding in the broken a means to make something joined that questions certainties and invites new, and perhaps better relations. Jimmie Durham's practice that I have discussed in this book creates for me an art of relations through which to think about, sense, imagine, and work toward expanding networks of kinship and flourishing. I hope that you, my reader, have such an art of relations in your life with others too.

References

Alfonsi, Sharyn. 2020. "Early Results from 174 Flint Children Exposed to Lead during Water Crisis Shows 80% of Them Will Require Special Education Services." *60 Minutes*, March 15, 2020. https://www.cbsnews.com/news/flint-water-crisis-effect-on-children-60-minutes-2020-03-15/.

Alves, Maria Thereza, and Jimmie Durham. 2018. Artist Statement for *The Middle Earth*, Institut d'art Contemporain, Villeurbanne, March 2–May 27, 2018.

Bloch, Ernst, and Mark Ritter. 1976. "Dialectics and Hope." *New German Critique* 9: 3–10. https://doi.org/10.2307/487685.

Chen, Mel Y. 2012. *Animacies: Biopolitics, Racial Mattering, and Queer Affect*. Durham, NC and London: Duke University Press. https://doi.org/10.1215/9780822395447.

Coole, Diana, and Samantha Frost, eds. 2010. *New Materialisms: Ontology, Agency, and Politics*. Durham, NC and London: Duke University Press. https://doi.org/10.1215/9780822392996.

Damrosch, David. 1991. "The Aesthetics of Conquest: Aztec Poetry before and after Cortés." *Representations* 33: 101–20. https://doi.org/10.2307/2928759.

de la Cadena, Marisol, and Mario Blaser, eds. 2018. *A World of Many Worlds*. Durham, NC and London: Duke University Press. https://doi.org/10.1215/9781478004318.

Durham, Jimmie. 2014. *Waiting to Be Interrupted: Selected Writings, 1993–2012*. Edited by Jean Fisher. Milan: Mousse Publishing; Antwerp: M HKA.

The Editors of Encyclopaedia Britannica. 2019. "Wire." *Encyclopædia Britannica*, January 29, 2019. https://www.britannica.com/technology/wire.

Grinberg, Kevin. 2013. "History and Grandeur of Murano Glass Chandeliers." *Glass of Venice*, July 10, 2013. https://www.glassofvenice.com/blog/2013/07/history-and-grandeur-of-murano-glass-chandeliers/.

Miyazaki, Hirokazu. 2004. *The Method of Hope: Anthropology, Philosophy, and Fijian Knowledge*. Stanford, CA: Stanford University Press.

Peterson, Jeanette Favrot, and Kevin Terraciano, eds. 2019. *The Florentine Codex: An Encyclopedia of the Nahua World in Sixteenth-Century Mexico*. Austin: University of Texas Press.

Porter, Aichele K. 1989. "Paul Klee's 'Flower Myth': Themes from German Romanticism Reinterpreted." *Notes in the History of Art* 8, no. 3: 16–21. https://doi.org/10.1086/sou.8.3.23202684.

Queen Mary, University of London. 2011. "Through the Looking Glass: Physicists Solve Age-Old Problem." *Phys*, October 17, 2011. https://phys.org/news/2011-10-glass-physicists-age-old-problem.html.

Rossell, Cecilia. 2005. "Which Was the Most Precious Color for the Aztecs and Why?" *Mexicolore*. https://www.mexicolore.co.uk/aztecs/ask-experts/which-was-the-most-precious-colour-for-the-aztecs-and-why.

Thompson, Peter. 2013. "The Frankfurt School, Part 6: Ernst Bloch and the Principle of Hope." *The Guardian*, April 29, 2013. https://www.theguardian.com/commentisfree/belief/2013/apr/29/frankfurt-school-ernst-bloch-principle-of-hope.

Index

For Product Safety Concerns and Information please contact our EU
representative GPSR@taylorandfrancis.com
Taylor & Francis Verlag GmbH, Kaufingerstraße 24, 80331 München, Germany